A
PRIMER
OF
BOOK
COLLECTING

A
PRIMER
OF
BOOK
COLLECTING

Third Revised Edition

■

by

John T. Winterich

and

David A. Randall

■

BELL PUBLISHING COMPANY   NEW YORK

CONTENTS

TO

EMILY WINTERICH

AND

POLLY RANDALL

PREFACE TO THE FIRST EDITION

This book does not presuppose on the part of the reader any technical acquaintance with book collecting as distinguished from book accumulating. One must, of course, be an accumulator—the estate is wholly honorable—before one can be a collector. In all that follows, therefore, some cultural background is assumed—some recognition of the distinction between Thackeray and G. P. R. James, between Mrs. Browning and Mrs. E. D. E. N. Southworth, between Emerson and Brann the Iconoclast.

It is true that a man may possess himself of Parts I, II, and III of *The Dynasts*—Part I having the 1903 title page—and yet have no clearer conception of Hardy's philosophy than that he wrote several gloomy novels and considerable rather gloomier poetry. There is, of course, plenty of room for bunk and the veneer of culture to creep into the pastime of book collecting—which, in the instance cited, is certainly nothing against *The Dynasts*, any more than the glory of a Rembrandt is dimmed by its presence in the salon of a self-made magnate who, in his honest heart of hearts, prefers Bud Fisher. But this discussion is verging perilously close to answering the question "Why collect books?"—an argument into which this writer and this book resolutely decline to be drawn.

Except to this extent: The lure of book collecting is the lure of the chase; it had its roots, like the lure of collecting anything, in the brain of that dim ancestor who one morning, in pursuit of the day's food supply, discovered a joy in the hunt itself which was something apart from the pleasure of consuming the quarry.

To rail at wealthy book collectors, however, is merely to violate that commandment which, certainly for the sake of emphasis, is writ last in the Decalogue. For, passing over the occasional exception of the man who makes his own—witness Blake, Stevenson, and William Morris—there are only three ways of obtaining books: by gift, by thievery (of which the most heinous form is borrowing), and by purchase. To buy books—the most logical means of acquiring them—requires money; to buy a Gutenberg Bible, at current market quotations, would require the rather comfortable fortune of one hundred thousand dollars and more—undoubtedly more. That is one extreme. The other is the secondhand dealer's five-cent box. Between them lies every book in creation.

It is safe to make the generalization that ninety-nine first editions out of a hundred (not including, obviously, the most eagerly or even the moderately sought for) now sell for rather less than they did as new books—which is another way of saying that book collecting can be no less a poor man's diversion than a rich man's. For anyone who can afford an occasional new book can afford an occasional old book, and while a book can sometimes be collected at the source as it drops from the press (or, more properly, from the binder's hands), most collector's items are not new.

These, however, are concerns for more leisurely discussion than a brief foreword should be expected to put up with. It remains only to say a defensive word on the vexed question of price. In the pages that follow the writer occasionally tires of surrounding every dollar sign with elaborate qualifying phrases, and sometimes makes the flat and unrelieved statement that such a book is worth such a figure. In every case, however, the price given represents either an actual transaction (which figure a subsequent actual transaction may make appear ridiculous), or the figure at which at least one reputable dealer is holding a copy for sale, or the result of an averaging of values and prices by the writer, generally made with the help of persons who know more about it than himself. It must be remembered, too, that the element of condition must be taken into account whenever a dollar sign is coupled with the title of a rare book.

JOHN T. WINTERICH

Ossining, New York

PREFACE TO THE THIRD REVISION

This book first appeared in 1927, John T. Winterich, author, and was reissued in a revised edition in 1935. I was privileged to assist in its second revision in 1946—the title then recorded John T. Winterich as author, "in collaboration with David A. Randall." Two decades later, in 1966, in this third revision, my name is, through his insistence, listed as co-author. (This will cause enormous confusion in library catalogues, I trust.)

I like to think of John's book as a frigate, recalling Emily Dickinson's "There is no frigate like a book." This book is what its title states, a *Primer*. It was never meant to be a *Ship of the Line*. The *Oxford English Dictionary* offers the following definition of a frigate from P. Barry's *Dockyard Economy:* "A ship of more than usually heavy scantling with a variety of foreign timber judiciously distributed." The soundness of the scantling is evidenced by the fact that, four decades after launching, the *Primer* sets forth on a new voyage. I trust the "foreign timbers" inserted by the second-in-command are "judiciously distributed."

DAVID A. RANDALL

Bloomington, Indiana

PART I

■

THE
QUARRY

■

■

FIRST
EDITIONS
AND
BLOOD
RELATIONS

■

The principal book collector in America is the United States Government. Since 1870, two copies of every publication for which copyright is sought must be deposited in the Library of Congress; before that it ˉwas only necessary to register a printed title page. Not every author or editor, however, seeks the privilege of Federal protection, nor are all books sent there permanently preserved, so that the Library of Congress is by no means an all-inclusive assemblage even of the books published in America since the copyright law became effective. Wealth and taste could hardly improve upon the eclecticism represented in the Pierpont Morgan Library in New York, whose trustees would be happy to declare a public holiday if they might lay hands on a copy of *The Bay Psalm Book*, printed (after a fashion) by Stephen Daye at Cambridge, Massachusetts, in 1640. The remarkably fine collection of the works of Lewis Carroll, assembled over many years by Morris L. Parrish of Philadelphia and left by him to Princeton, along with his other collections of Victorian authors, lacked the true first edition of *Alice's Adventures in Wonderland,* published at London in 1865. This was so rigorously suppressed by its author owing to his being displeased with its presswork (suppression does not always imply salaciousness) that only a handful of copies of it are known to be in existence. Mr. Parrish's possession of Carroll's own copy of the second London edition, 1866, extensively corrected in the author's own autograph (treasure enough, one would think), never quite consoled him for the missing first edition.

In collecting books, specialization is an immediate necessity—and specialization must be carried to a fine point to ensure any hope of completeness. The William Faulkner enthusiast should be able to fill many of his needs by sending a want list to half a dozen dealers--and then spend several years awaiting a perfect copy of his first book, *The Marble Faun* (1924), which is poetry, and was reprinted only in 1965. *The Scarlet Letter* of 1850 must sooner or later fall to the lot of the Hawthorne collector who is willing to forego one or two suits of clothes, if necessary, in order to acquire it, but he may have to deny himself a country estate to gain a *Fanshawe* of 1828, and can count himself lucky indeed among mortals if he ever has an opportunity to spend the money. With a first printing of 15,000 copies, Theodore Dreiser's *An American Tragedy* (1925) is not likely ever to command an excessive premium over its published price, but his *Sister Carrie* (1900) is already established as one of the scarcest American novels of its generation, and, unless Mr. Dreiser's place in letters is severely discounted by posterity, the demand for the original *Sister Carrie* will always exceed the supply—a condition that is reflected with considerable accuracy in the auction rooms and the dealers' catalogues.

If one wants to read *Sister Carrie* he can, of course, buy a copy of the latest paperback printing for a dollar or so, brand new, dust wrapper and all. If one wants to read *The Scarlet Letter*, he should be able to get some edition of it for twenty-five cents in any secondhand bookstore. In the preceding paragraph first editions only are considered. And thereby hangs a tale—the chief tale in the whole chronicle of book collecting.

The first edition, indeed, is so strongly accented in contemporary collecting that the noncollector is likely to regard it as the whole story. Actually it is far from being the whole story. While a collector-library which contained no first edition would probably be harder to assemble than one composed exclusively of first editions, and while the assembling of such a library would be a willful, frustrate, and inept pursuit, still a library containing only a small proportion of firsts —say 10 percent—could well be a valuable and useful assemblage, and might well represent the expenditure of more intelligence (and considerably less funds) than a collection consisting wholly of firsts. When, a little later, specific collecting fields are taken up, it will be in order to discuss this problem in more detail.

Both collector and bookseller mean, by a first edition, a first appearance of a written work in book form. This, of course, may not be its first appearance in print. What ought the collector do about magazines? At present he does little enough about them, but the time may come when they will have a place of honor on his shelves. The sentimental distinction between a book and a magazine consists in the fact that an author must share an issue of a magazine with other authors, whereas in most instances he is likely to have a book to himself. There is, in addition, a practical distinction that outweighs the sentimental. Twelve issues of a magazine containing as many installments of a serial story take up probably three times as much shelfroom as does the same story in book form. Books are bulky enough objects in themselves, and the average collector is content to draw the line at books.

But there are significant exceptions. Thus, the issues of *Harper's Magazine* containing Du Maurier's *Trilby* have collection interest apart from the book itself, because Whistler was caricatured (or so considered himself) in certain of the author's illustrations which appeared with *Trilby* as a serial, and was described in the text in terms which he did not regard as flattering, and the offending portrayals, graphic and verbal, do not appear in *Trilby* the book.

When *The Autocrat of the Breakfast-Table* initiated its serial appearance with the first number (November, 1857) of *The Atlantic Monthly* it began, as it still begins: "I was just going to say, when I was interrupted." The interruption extended back to February, 1832, when, in *The New-England Magazine* for that month, the second of two papers (the earlier had appeared the previous November) called *The Autocrat of the Breakfast Table* (note the absence of the hyphen) had been published. The mere lapse of time and the subsequent resumption of the series ought, perhaps, be sufficient excuse for making *The New-England Magazine* an affair of moment to the Holmes collector, but there is a weightier reason. The two *New-England* papers, save for three brief extracts which Holmes incorporated in the preface, were never included in the *Autocrat* in book form. "They will not," said Holmes, "be reprinted here, nor, as I hope, anywhere," a hope not fulfilled.

We have said that one argument against the collecting of periodicals is the fact that an author must share an issue of a magazine with other authors. Yet this may be an advantage rather than a disadvantage, a distinction rather than a lack of it. The earliest number of *The Atlantic Monthly*, just referred to, contains not only the first installment of the resurrected *Autocrat*, but four poems and an essay by Emerson, two poems and a department by Lowell, a poem by Whittier, and a short story by Harriet Beecher Stowe. What would the proprietor of a twentieth-century magazine be willing to offer for such a roster of contributors?

Ninety-five years later, Ernest Hemingway's *The Old Man and the Sea* first appeared in *Life* magazine (September 1, 1952). The Hemingway enthusiast will want, for his collection, not the newsstand issue but an advance number with a note on the cover reading "First run copy, not completely made ready."

These examples explain themselves, but it would be possible to adduce other instances of periodical issues which are established collector items in spite of the fact that they frequently lack the prestige of logic to support their status. Thus, "The Star-Spangled Banner," under its original designation of "Defence of Fort McHenry," appeared, but by no means for the first time, in *The Analectic Magazine* for November, 1814. Preceding the stanzas was an extended note which began: "These lines have been already published in several of our newspapers; they may still, however, be new to many of our readers. Besides, we think that their merit entitles them to preservation in some more permanent form than the columns of a daily paper." The *Analectic* version, therefore, was a reprint, and far from the first reprint, of a national anthem, yet Volume IV of the *Analectic* is an occasional visitor to the auction room and receives a hearty welcome, especially if it is in its original wrappers. The first printing of the anthem with music (Baltimore, 1814) can be determined (if you are lucky enough to find one—only twelve are known) by a misprint in the subtitle: "A Pariotic Song."

Harriet Beecher Stowe's famed *Uncle Tom's Cabin; or, Life Among the Lowly,* was written for a leading Abolitionist weekly, the *National Era,* published in Washington, D. C., of which John Greenleaf Whittier was Corresponding Editor.

The first *Star Spangled Banner*
with music, one of twelve recorded copies.

The first chapter appeared June 5, 1851. The original intention was to conclude it in a few numbers, as a short story, but so widespread was the interest it aroused, and so intense grew the conviction of the author as she wrote it that she had undertaken a holy mission, that it ran on until the following April and was then issued as a two-volume novel.

Nor is it necessary that a periodical date back to 1857 or 1832 or 1814 or earlier in order to be an exemplar of established collector desirability. *The Seven Arts* survived only from November, 1916, through October, 1917, but it is eagerly sought (and usually in vain) by collectors of modern American literature.

The instances just cited are wholly casual and arbitrary; a list of desirable periodicals, American and English, could be extended to tediousness. The beginning collector must survey the field for himself and determine whether or not it has a particular appeal to him. He will probably find that his collecting interest will operate in reverse—he will begin with books, and perhaps, but not inevitably, he will work back to periodicals. One point must be stressed before consideration of the magazine (which has perhaps been disproportionately accented already) is abandoned: book texts and magazine texts often differ in minor, sometimes in major, details, and a rich field of exploration lies open to the possessor of both periodical and definitive versions.

Gordon N. Ray, chairman of the John Simon Guggenheim Memorial Foundation, stressed this point in a 1964 survey of "Bibliographical Resources for the Study of Nineteenth Century English Fiction" where he recorded 46 copies of the first book edition of Robert Louis Stevenson's immortal *Treasure Island* (1883) to only three copies of its original serialization in *Young Folks* (October, 1881–January, 1882). And Hardy's *Tess of the D'Urbervilles'* first appearance was in *The Graphic* magazine (1891) with illustrations, some

THE ♥ NATIONAL ERA.

G. BAILEY, EDITOR AND PROPRIETOR; JOHN G. WHITTIER, CORRESPONDING EDITOR.

VOL. V.—NO. 23.

WASHINGTON, THURSDAY, JUNE 5, 1851.

WHOLE NO. 231.

THE NATIONAL ERA.

WASHINGTON, JUNE 2, 1851.

UNCLE TOM'S CABIN.

LIFE AMONG THE LOWLY.

The National Era, with the original appearance of *Uncle Tom's Cabin.*

very powerful and mostly unreproduced to this day. He concludes, in our opinion correctly, that "the student who sees the magazine as it was issued will gain an altogether clearer notion of what the concept of the story's first publication in fact was than he will from a bound volume." An excellent essay on this whole subject is Graham Pollard's "Serial Fiction" in *New Paths in Book Collecting* (1934); nothing of comparable importance has been done since.

Such a field of exploration, obviously, is not available to the collector who regards the units of his collection as museum pieces, and if their value goes into large figures he is likely so to regard them. This state of affairs frequently gives rise to much mirth among noncollectors, who like to picture the wretched plight of the man surrounded by thousands of books who yet has nothing to read. There are collectors who do read their books, whether the books have cost them one dollar or a thousand, but such assiduity is not typical. Nor does it follow that, because a collector of Stevenson or Mark Twain lets his firsts remain on his shelves, consulting them only at rare intervals and exhibiting them at rarer, he is wholly unacquainted with the writings of Stevenson or Mark Twain. In fact, unless the collector is the utterest of copycats, he began to collect Stevenson or Mark Twain in the first place because of a sentimental interest in them gained through a previous acquaintance with their work. The nub of the business is that a costly rare book is precisely a museum piece. The beginner, however, is likely to feel more at home with books which represent an investment of such modest dimensions that, if he should drop one and shatter its spine or loosen its hinges, the act would not represent the equivalent of flinging a life-insurance policy into the fireplace. Many superb collections of books, both public and private, are definitely for use; it is certainly wisest for the beginner to confine himself not only to books which he wants to use but to books which he feels he safely may use.

Charles Lamb—the perfect instance of a great book lover with little money to spend in book buying—observed that first editions were not so rare as tenth editions. *Vanity Fairs*, *Ben-Hurs*, and *Gone With the Winds* do not appear every day—unfortunately for publishers. The search for best sellers or even good sellers entails a vast and perpetual gamble with poor sellers and nonsellers. And poor sellers and nonsellers rarely emerge from the distinguished poverty of first editions.

"Does anyone collect So-and-so?" we once asked a rare-book dealer.

"We do, but our customers don't," he answered.

And another dealer, whom we heard being vainly besought to buy a book that the would-be seller proclaimed to be very scarce, replied: "Yes, it is scarce, but people who want it are scarcer."

An important canon of book collecting can here be set down:

The fact that a given book is a first edition does not necessarily imply that it has any cultural, intellectual, historical, sentimental, and therefore collector appeal.

What first editions, then, do have collector appeal? Those first editions, obviously, that collectors want, for the law of supply and demand is the fundamental economic principle of book collecting.

It can be said that, without exception, any book that has survived the test of time, or any book, however little known, the writer of which has survived the test of time or seems likely to survive it, has definite value in first edition.

An author's best-known book, or his best book, is not likely to be so costly as certain examples of his earlier and presumably less-known work. Kipling's two *Jungle Books* (1894–1895) will survive long after everyone (except collectors and dealers) has forgotten that he ever had a youthful hand in a pamphlet called *Schoolboy Lyrics* (1881), yet today the *Jungle Books* can be obtained for less than a tenth of the cost of a copy of *Schoolboy Lyrics*—and the *Jungle Books* are not cheap. Thackeray's *Henry Esmond* (1852) in the original three volumes is not difficult of acquisition, whereas a copy of *King Glumpus* (1837), a one-act play by John Barrow—ever hear of him?—to which Thackeray contributed three colored drawings, has gone into four figures at auction. But if Kipling had written nothing after *Schoolboy Lyrics,* and Thackeray had abandoned pen and pencil after *King Glumpus,* those productions would be worthless today.

Take, again, *The Bay Psalm Book,* already referred to, printed under devout Pilgrim auspices twenty years after the *Mayflower* reached that stern and rockbound coast which became the springboard of American culture. John Winterich wrote in the original edition of this *Primer* (1927) that if another copy of it should ever come to light it would certainly change hands at public sale at a higher figure than a native book had ever attained before. Why? Published in 1640, it has absolutely no value on account of its age—in the abstract, indeed, it is a rather new book. (The theory exists, among people who know nothing about it, that an old book is a valuable book, which is quite true if one is an accurate judge of age. Mention will be made later in this chapter of a book which has sold at $3,150 solely on account of its age—it was published in 1848.) *The Bay Psalm Book* is not a first edition of the Psalms, which had been put in type hundreds of times before 1640. It is not valuable as an example of fine printing, for physically it is a mediocre product. It is valuable only— and for reason enough—because it is the oldest surviving book printed in what is now the United States, and because only eleven copies, of which only two are perfect, are known to exist. A pioneer book, regardless of date, author, contents, or quality of printing, never goes begging.

Winterich, reports Randall, proved a true prophet, for a

copy of *The Bay Psalm Book* did appear at auction in New York City in 1947. This was the Crowninshield-Stevens-Brinley-Vanderbilt-Whitney copy (books, as well as horses, often have pedigrees). It is the only copy ever to appear at public sale, and it appeared twice: first in the remarkable George Brinley sale in 1878, where it brought $1,200, and was purchased by the late Cornelius Vanderbilt. His descendants put it up for sale (the proceeds were given to a hospital), and it brought $151,000, the highest price ever paid at public auction for a printed book. It is now at Yale.

The examples that have been given fall within the category of books of definite literary or historical significance—and the history of which a book is significant may be social, literary, technical, racial, local, or whatnot. First books on beekeeping, cooking, navigation, fishing, Christian Science, equestrianism, smoking, boxing; early—really early—grammars, arithmetics, geographies; early almanacs, timetables, directories—these, and early books in a thousand other categories, enjoy a valuation fantastically in excess of anything their creators might have dreamed. A collection of early dime novels attained the dignity of glass cases in the New York Public Library. Of recent years great interest has been shown in the collecting of science fiction and detective fiction. Vincent Starrett has written lyrically and accurately of Conan Doyle's first Sherlock Holmes story *A Study in Scarlet*, which appeared in Beeton's Christmas *Annual* for 1887: "That lurid paper-back is today one of the rarest books of modern times—a keystone sought by discriminating collectors in every part of the earth." A London dealer not long since issued a fascinating catalogue of early books on aviation. We would say that there is an interesting field for the collector in atomic bombia save for our certainty that he must have discovered it already. Whatever a man's hobby, he can parallel it—or his trade, his profession, even his pet aversion—

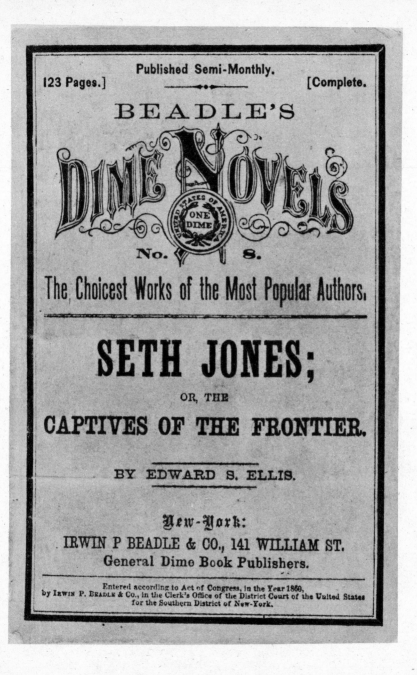

Published Semi-Monthly.

123 Pages.]   [Complete.

BEADLE'S

Dime Novels

ONE DIME

NO. 8.

The Choicest Works of the Most Popular Authors.

SETH JONES;

OR, THE

CAPTIVES OF THE FRONTIER.

BY EDWARD S. ELLIS.

New-York:

IRWIN P BEADLE & CO., 141 WILLIAM ST.
General Dime Book Publishers.

One of Beadle's famous Dime Novels.

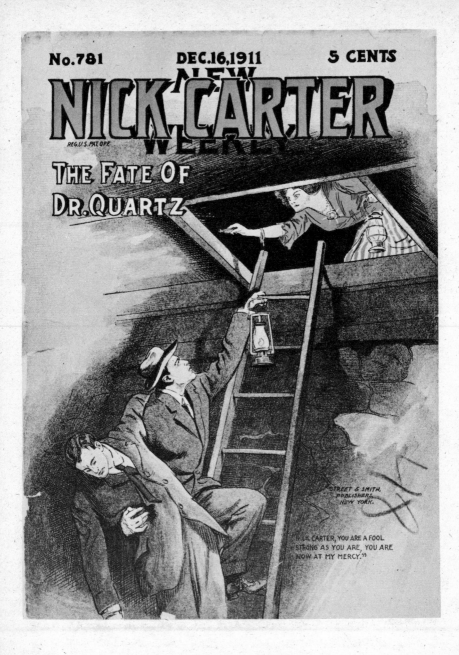

No. 781   DEC. 16, 1911   5 CENTS

NEW

NICK CARTER

REG. U.S. PAT. OFF.

WEEKLY

The Fate Of Dr. Quartz

STREET & SMITH,
PUBLISHERS.
NEW YORK.

"NICK CARTER, YOU ARE A FOOL
STRONG AS YOU ARE, YOU ARE
NOW AT MY MERCY."

A typical Nick Carter.

in book collecting. Most book collecting is, naturally, in the field of pure literature. (We say "pure" in no moral sense, though the collecting of impure literature, or erotica, sometimes more stealthily labeled facetiae, has its devotees.)

The great names in the noble chronicle of English letters command, in first edition, values that are an accurate reflection of that nobility. Indeed, as the pageant moves back to Chaucer's self, imperfections—even occasionally of numerous lacking leaves—are overlooked, and later-than-first editions as well as violently repaired and "made-up" copies begin to acquire a prestige of their own.

In 1962 Indiana University sold at auction in New York certain duplicate volumes, among them Chaucer's *The Canterbury Tales,* printed by William Caxton at Westminster in 1478, the first edition of the first major literary classic in English done by England's first printer. It was seriously defective; having 290 of 374 leaves only, but it brought $47,500 (it had last sold in the Frank Hogan sale in 1946 for $13,000). Even more astonishing was the sale by auction in London in 1965 of the first illustrated edition of *The Canterbury Tales,* also printed by Caxton, about 1484, lacking 36 leaves, for $84,000. Also in 1965, and again at London, an imperfect copy (lacking among other things seven of the eight preliminary leaves, including the title page) of the first edition of the first complete English Bible, translated by Miles Coverdale (Marburg, 1535), fetched $44,800. Thus less than perfect copies of the truly great books command substantial prices. This is particularly true, inevitably, of Shakespeare. It would be impossible today for a collector, no matter how affluent, to assemble a comprehensive collection of his works in first editions. One needs only to look at Henrietta Bartlett's *A Census of Shakespeare's Plays in Quarto* to see how astonishingly few of the extant copies are in private hands, and many of these have since gravitated to institutions.

It is all very discouraging. The beginning—or, worse yet,
the unbegun—collector who is devoted to Shakespeare and
would be glad to collect books if he could only collect Shakespeare must toss up his hands.

But must he?

Here are ten departments of Shakespearian investigation
in each of which the collector can spend years—and comparatively little money:

(1) Shakespearian criticism in America.

(2) The history of Shakespearian production in America—
general, or limited to a single community. A diligent collector could soon make himself an authority on Shakespeare
on the San Francisco or the Chicago stage.

(3) Biographies and autobiographies of American actors
famous for their successes (or even for their failures) in
Shakespearian roles.

(4) American-edited school readers containing selections
from Shakespeare (preferably to a certain date).

(5) American-edited anthologies ditto.

(6) American novels deriving their titles from Shakespeare.

(7) Poetical tributes to Shakespeare by Americans.

(8) The history of the study of Shakespeare in American
schools and colleges.

(9) America and the Baconian heresy. And, of course,

(10) American editions of Shakespeare.

We stress the national adjective in these suggestions not
as an instance of spread-eagleism but because these notes
are designed for collectors in America, and it is helpful,

though not essential, for the collector to be near his source of supply. Reading English for American in the above list, the collector will find the ground either too well covered already or far too extensive, but he can substitute French, German, Polish, what he will, and enjoy good hunting.

Just as the first editions of the Elizabethans, and of their immediate precursors and successors, are likely to command until the end of time prices in keeping with the spaciousness of that ample day, so will many of the first editions of every great English (or American, or French, or German, or any other) author sell in general at figures which put them beyond the reach of the average collector. The collector of modest means is perforce a collector of modest books, but an intelligently assembled library of modest books can be much more than a modest collection. And while the run-of-the-shelves collector may not be able to mortgage a decade's income for the possession of sets of Lamb, Shelley, Keats, Dickens, Poe, and Hawthorne in first edition, he can parallel, in his chosen field, the suggestions that have been offered the Shakespearian student. His supreme literary interest, let us say, is Dickens, though he can never hope to acquire a perfect *Posthumous Papers of the Pickwick Club* in the monthly parts in which it was originally issued. Even if he is willing to take his Dickens in American firsts instead of English firsts he will have to prepare for a substantial outlay, and, outlay aside, he will find the search actually more difficult. But if he confines his activity to one (or merely to part of one) of the following spheres of Dickensian research he will find his endeavors and discoveries far more exciting than if he commissioned a bookseller to acquire every Dickens first for him, money no object:

(1) American fiction published during his lifetime containing allusions to Dickens, his novels, or his characters.

(2) Contemporary guides and local histories of the area covered by Dickens in his first visit to the United States, using *American Notes* as a basis.

(3) Dramatized versions of the novels.

(4) American literary productions directly inspired by Dickens, such as Elisha Bartlett's *Simple Settings in Verse from Mr. Dickens's Gallery* (Boston, 1855) and *The Mystery of Edwin Drood Complete* (Brattleboro, Vermont, 1873), the "completeness" having been provided "by the spirit pen of Charles Dickens through a medium."

(5) Dickens and the pulpit—published sermons by American ministers inspired by him, his two visits, his books.

(6) Dickens sheet music.

(7) The American engravings of Dickens's illustrations.

(8) Every procurable edition of a single Dickens title.

(9) Accounts by Americans of visits to or interviews with Dickens, from C. Edwards Lester's *The Glory and the Shame of England* (New York, 1841) to T. C. Evans's *Of Many Men* (New York, 1888) and beyond.

(10) Imitations of Dickens, or of a single Dickens novel, such as *Pickwick Abroad; or The Tour in France,* by G. W. M. Reynolds (London, 1839), and *Pickwick in America! Detailing all the Remarkable Adventures of Taat* [sic] *Illustrious Individual and His Learned Companions, in the United States, Extraordinary Jonathanisms, Collected by Mr. Snodgrass, and the Sayings, Doings, and Mems, of the Facetious Sam Weller. Edited by "Bos"* (London, about 1842).

Lest this chapter, which set out to discuss first editions, be regarded as having blandly turned its back on them, let it here be stated that there will be considerable further discus-

sion of firsts both in this chapter and in those that follow it.
But we want to make it clear that those collectors who cannot hope to possess the great firsts can at any rate touch
the hem of their writers' garments.

What has been said concerning English literature applies
equally, in kind if not always in degree, to American literature. We are a young country—so far. Our books are much
fresher than England's. None of them north of Mexico bears
a date so early as 1623—the year of the Shakespeare First
Folio. Being fresher, our books have had fewer opportunities
to wear out or to get lost; we are notorious for our tendency
to conflagrations, but we have had no Great Fire of London
to sweep through our largest publishing district and to create, as a by-product, a fantastic scarcity in certain titles. Our
closest approach to Shakespeare, collector-wise, is Edgar
Allan Poe, and there are plenty of persons who are active
and about today whose grandfathers were born before Poe's
first book appeared. It was called *Tamerlane and Other
Poems. By a Bostonian* (Boston, 1827) and while it is not yet
anything like so costly as a perfect First Folio, it may be one
day, and it is a much scarcer book. Twelve copies, not all of
them perfect, are known, and the book has sold for as much
as $25,000. Poe's second book, *Al Aaraaf, Tamerlane, and
Minor Poems* (Baltimore, 1829) is not so expensive as *Tamerlane*, but it is almost as rare. So, too, is his third work,
Poems (New York, 1831), all copies of which are marked
"Second Edition" on the title page, a mere fiction possibly
designed to stimulate an appearance of popularity which
Poe did not at that time enjoy. This is the so-called "West
Point" edition as it is dedicated to the cadets there, of whom
Poe was no longer one. With these three titles the Poe col-
lector has only begun, though it is more likely that he will
cap the arch of his collection with them, if he is lucky and
has contrived to evade bankruptcy.

The late Carroll A. Wilson, who formed a remarkable collection of rarities, prefaced the Poe section of the catalogue of his books with the note that "it is probably supererogatory to put it down but I do not own the first edition of either *Tamerlane, Al Aaraaf* or *Poems,* 1831!!!" Yet he did acquire a Poe collection distinguished by one of three known autographs of the youthful printer of *Tamerlane,* the only recorded copy of the magazine appearance of "The Mystery of Marie Roget" in its original state (1842–1843), and a fine run of comparable material.

The Poe touch universally transmutes paper and ink into gold. We have alluded to magazines as collector's items—where Poe is concerned the magazine as a collector's item has long had the prestige of desirability and value behind it, and ever will have.

But even in the instance of Poe it is possible for the inexperienced and impecunious collector to assemble a group of books of scholarly importance and value. No private collector, so far as we know, is today in avid search of the first editions of George Bush, John W. Francis, George B. Cheever, Ralph Hoyt, Piero Maroncelli, Laughton Osborn, James Lawson, or Prosper M. Wetmore—the list could be extended, not indefinitely, but certainly to thirty or forty. All were writers who received Poe's critical attention in *The Literati*—some his fulsome praise, others his venom and scorn, still others a just and enduring appraisal of their merits or demerits.

Far too often Poe was an *ad hominem* critic, but this condition, deplorable though it may be in the abstract, makes the minor writers whom he discussed, no less than the major, the more attractive to the collector. Take, for instance, Dr. Francis: "He speaks in a loud, clear, hearty tone, dogmatically, with his head thrown back and his chest out; never waits for an introduction to anybody; slaps a perfect stranger on the back and calls him 'Doctor' or 'Learned

Theban'; pats every lady on the head, and (if she be pretty and *petite*) designates her by some such title as 'My Pocket Edition of the Lives of the Saints.'" Does, or does not, this fragment from Poe's six-hundred-word account of Dr. Francis lend a touch of interest to the doctor's *Inaugural Dissertation on Memory* (1811), his *Cases of Morbid Anatomy* (1814), or his *Address before the New York Academy of Medicine on the Election of Professor Mott* (1849)? Some twenty titles are essential to a set of Dr. Francis in first edition, and their assembling might be the toil of years.

Or consider James Lawson. Poe devoted a mere paragraph to him, but there was a sting in its tail: "He is much in the society of authors and booksellers, converses fluently, tells a good story, is of social habits, and, with no taste whatever, is quite enthusiastic on all topics pertaining to taste." The characterization, whether just or not, must at least inspire some slight curiosity toward Lawson's *Tales and Sketches by a Cosmopolite* (1830) and his *Giordano, a Tragedy* (1832). Would an inspection of these and others of Lawson's survivals disclose him as possessing "no taste whatever"? The answer, whether yes or no, would have a definite bearing on the infallibility or lack of it of Poe's judgment, and to that extent *Giordano* is an authentic collateral Poe item. We suggest, as a test case, that the intending collector read the accounts of both Francis and Lawson in the brothers Duyckinck's *Cyclopaedia of American Literature* (1855) and in the *Dictionary of American Biography*, and see whether his interest in them quickens into a desire for their *opera omnia*.

First editions of the great mid-century New England group —Emerson, Hawthorne, Whittier, Longfellow, Holmes, Thoreau—have enjoyed a varied collecting history. Of the rarer items, many (in particular Hawthorne's anonymous *Fanshawe* of 1828) come high and come seldom, but the enthusiast who wants a representative collection of their minor items can acquire many of them for the price each of an average new book. Until quite recently a comparatively small expenditure would have purchased a majority of the works of each of the group, but that day is gone, and the great New Englanders are now firmly fixed in the collector's hierarchy. In general it may be said that book collecting is as much subject to the whims of style as clothes collecting, a condition which the collector may indignantly deplore, but of which he can take wise advantage.

Modern authors, British and American, have their devoted followings, and offer the collector an intellectual gamble that should appeal to his sporting instincts. It is not likely that the exalted positions of Shakespeare, Milton, Poe, Hawthorne, and Dickens will ever be compromised. But in judging contemporaries one cannot be so sure. What will be the fame of Ernest Hemingway a century hence? His first editions sell at present for prices that are ridiculously excessive or ridiculously cheap, according to whether one regards the Hemingway following as a company of ignorant fanatics or as torchbearing prophets of a glory that will endure through the ages in the chronicle of American letters. Was Sherwood Anderson a clownish poseur whose only contribution to art was a psychopathic species of punctuation, or was he an authentic spokesman of a big-boyish America which common minds without the vision fail to comprehend? Was James Branch Cabell a beautiful stylist and the most subtly ironic genius of his country and generation, or a mere flash-in-the-pan smart aleck whose name has already been forgotten? Should one characterize D. H. Lawrence as a charlatan with a flair for highbrow pornography, or as an incisive student of character in the terms of an accurate science of psycho-analysis? Which was Theodore Dreiser, the greatest American novelist of his time or a ponderous and blundering exuder of words?

The reader is invited to continue the list as he sees fit. He will acknowledge, we think, that in the case of most of the authors cited a true judgment may not lie in either extreme, but somewhere between. Just where? Posterity will have the pleasure of answering that question. We of today, however, can guess, basing our estimates on the run of critical opinion, the views of our friends, and our own judgments—especially our own judgments. (It may be worth noting here, in passing, that one must not look for catholicity of taste among collectors. One man's collecting meat is another's poison, and Heaven be praised that it is so.)

The collector of the books of contemporary and nearly contemporary authors—and, one might almost add, of not quite yet contemporary authors, so hot sometimes grows the pursuit—must have the courage of his convictions. He must, at any rate, have the courage, and his activities will be futile unless he has at least some shadow of conviction—and it must be his own conviction before anyone else's. In order to acquire conviction he will first of all read the books he collects (not necessarily the identical copies he collects), and having thus made a sample valuation, he will check it against such critical data as may be available. Often he will be able to find little enough of it, which will add both to the difficulty and to the pleasure of the game which he is playing. He will evaluate this critical data exactly as he evaluates the object of it. But his own summation must always be his supreme court.

Allusion has already been made to the book as a museum piece—to the problem of whether a collectible book is to be read or not to be read—and the subject can be, has always been, and always will be discussed at length. The nonreading book collector was first held up to scorn, in English at least, in 1509, when Richard Pynson of London issued *The Ship of Fools*—Alexander Barclay's translation of Sebastian Brandt's *Das Narrenschiff*, which had been published at

Basle in 1494 and had quickly been translated into Latin and French. Said Brandt's Fool Number One, by Barclay's rendering:

> I am the first fool of all the whole navie,
> To keep the poop, the helm and eke the sail,
> For this is in my mind, this one pleasure have I;
> Of books to have great plenty and aparayle.
> I take no wisdom by them, nor yet avail
> Nor them perceive not: and then I them despise.

The space intervening between Brandt's animadversions of 1494 and the present can be bridged at not too considerable intervals by other commentators on collector illiteracy— whoever wants to skim the subject will find it adequately summarized in Holbrook Jackson's *The Anatomy of Bibliomania* (1930).

But it is high time that the already heavily overweighted jape were definitely sunk. When book buyers and book borrowers in general begin to read in as heavy a proportion as book collectors it will be seasonable to revive it. There is more hokum in run-of-the-shop book buying and book borrowing than there has ever been in book collecting. What makes the genteel best seller? Intrinsic merit? A reputation based on what has gone before? An honest appreciation of artistic sincerity? Devotion to a durable novelty in style or treatment? None of these. The supreme inspiration, alas, is the age-old incentive to keep up with Literate Lizzie. This is the Thing to Do—this is the Book to Read. Or if not to read, at least to pretend familiarity with.

We have forgotten its name, or we should gladly give it here, which might be unjust, for the fault was less the writer's than his readers', if indeed there was fault in the writer at all. This was some years ago, when a certain title became the

Book of the Moment. A friend of ours, not so much humbly wishful to follow the crowd as he was convinced of the worth of the product by what he had heard and read of it, borrowed a copy of the Book from a lending library. From page 19 on it was unopened (or, as the uncollector would say, "uncut"). Yet the library record penciled on the last flyleaf proved that five "readers" had already borrowed it. Well, perhaps it was better to have tried and failed.

What any collector does with his books is primarily that collector's rather than society's affair. If he chooses to regard them as museum pieces, meticulously shrouding them in solander cases with felt-lined inner cloth wrappers, there is, and rightly, no one to say him nay—and in this event he assumes the added responsibility of delicately tending the cases as well as the books. If he is this sort of collector his heart will operate momentarily in reverse at the very thought of reading any of his treasures—he would as soon consider having the Bayeux Tapestry (if he owned it) made into a sport suit. He will govern the temperature and humidity—particularly the humidity—of his library as accurately as if it were an incubator stocked with phoenix eggs. To that library he may occasionally admit a handpicked visitor—not likely more than one visitor at a time, because two visitors are much more than twice as hard to watch as one—but not even to the guardianship of such a privileged and certified guest will he actually entrust one of his prizes.

At the other extreme is the collector who scorns solander and all other varieties of cases as diligently as he would repudiate handcuffs. His books, least and finest alike, bare their faces (rather than their shelfbacks) to the world with as bland ingenuousness as does the ceiling of the room that houses them. If the owner acquired them in dust jackets, the jackets have been thrown away as impertinences. Guests are welcome to the library, and are privileged to smoke, even

while examining books—and while they are examining books
no baleful and palpitant proprietary eye is fastened on them.
They may even read the books (only on the premises, one
hopes), for the owner himself has read them—as they are,
in first edition. He would not, indeed, dream of admitting
to his shelves a book that he did not intend to read or, having
once read, did not intend to read again.

In the foregoing discussion the accent has been largely on
authors—on the collecting of some*body* rather than the collecting of some*thing*. It is the logical line for the collector.
We know of no one with the patience or means to go in for
so voluminous a writer as Anonymous.

But one collects Bibles as Bibles, not as the works of a
whole group of writers from Moses to St. John. If research
should happen to prove that neither Moses nor St. John had
anything to do with its composition, the value of the Gutenberg Bible would hardly decrease thereby.

The Gutenberg Bible (Mainz, about 1455) is worth a comfortable fortune for two excellent reasons. It is the first book
ever printed from movable type. It is the first edition of the
supreme book of Christendom. The sentimental prestige implicit in those two statements is tremendous.

We can do no better here than to quote the late Seymour
de Ricci, leading bibliographer on the subject:

> *The Gutenberg Bible may be described without the
> slightest exaggeration not only as the earliest but also the
> greatest book in the world. It is the first book from the
> printing press, having been preceded only by a few trial
> pieces, single leaves, almanacs and grammatical booklets
> of which merely stray fragments remain.*
>
> *It is one of the most beautiful books ever printed: the
> quiet dignity of those twelve hundred and odd pages
> of dark stately type, the deep black of the ink, the broad-*

A page from the Gutenberg Bible,
the first large book printed
from movable metal type.

ness of the margins, the glossy crispness of the paper,
may have been equalled, but they have never been sur-
passed; and in its very cradle, the printers' art, thanks to
the Gutenberg Bible, shines forth indeed as an art as
much and more than as a craft.

Last but not least, The Gutenberg Bible is the first
edition of the Book of Books. The mere fact that in the
Rhine valley in 1450 the first book to be printed should
have been the Bible tells its own story. While Gutenberg
and Fust were actually at work, the fall of Constantinople
in 1453 announced the end of an old world and the dawn
of modern thought. Did Gutenberg realize that by
setting up the Holy Text in type he was heralding one
of the greatest movements of human thought in the history
of the civilized world?

The first copy to come to America (now at the New York
Public Library), was purchased by James Lenox in 1847 for
the then "mad price" of £500. It was insured for half a million dollars when shown at New York City's Golden Jubilee.
Henry Stevens of Vermont, the London bookseller, writing
in 1870 to George Brinley of Hartford, Connecticut, who
bought the second copy ever to cross the Atlantic, said:

Pray ponder for a moment to fully appreciate the rarity
and importance of this precious consignment from the Old
to the New World. It is not only the first Bible, but it is a
fine copy of the First Book ever printed. It was read in
Europe nearly half a century before America was discovered.
Therefore, in view of these considerations, please to sug-
gest to your Deputy at the seat of Customs to uncover his
head while in the presence of this first book and never for
a moment to turn his back upon it while the case is open.
Let no ungodly or thieving politician lay eyes or hands upon
it. The sight can now give him no good while the Bible
may suffer. Let none of Uncle Samuel's Custom House

*officials, or other men in or out of authority, see it without
first reverentially lifting their hats.*

Of the estimated 300 copies originally printed, 47 are
known today, the majority imperfect. America possesses 14
of these, Germany 11, Great Britain eight, France four, Italy
and Spain two each, and Austria, Denmark, Poland, Portugal,
Belgium, and Switzerland one each. All copies outside America, with one exception, are in permanent libraries, state
or institutional. The single exception is the copy privately
owned in Switzerland, formerly in the Imperial Library at
St. Petersburg, Russia, and sold in 1931 by order of the
Soviet government.

American copies are owned by the following libraries:
Congress; New York Public; General Theological Seminary,
New York; Pierpont Morgan, New York (3—how grand can
you get?); Yale; Harvard; Huntington; St. John's Seminary,
Camarillo, California; Indiana University. Three are in pri-
vate hands: The Carl Pforzheimer Trust, New York; William
H. Scheide, Princeton, New Jersey; and Arthur A. Houghton,
Jr., Queenstown, Maryland.

Dozens of other Bibles are valuable as early or special
editions, but this does not mean that the average old family
Bible is worth anything apart from its inconsiderable value
as so many pounds of waste paper. Any rare-book dealer can
recite a whole series of comic yet infinitely pathetic incidents
of callers who have come in to part with "very valuable" old
family Bibles as a last desperate effort to obtain money, and
who are at first highly indignant and then plunged into despair to learn that their precious volumes—genuinely precious
to them—are not worth the space they would occupy on the
dealer's shelves.

One can go in for Bibles, however, without troubling about
a Gutenberg—the likelihood of his getting one, even if the
collector can afford it, is extremely remote. Since several im-

perfect copies, however, have been "broken up," he can obtain a single leaf. Price will depend on condition and content and currently runs close to four figures. The collector should by all means read, as a delightful exegesis on the Bible as a collector's item, the first and title paper in A. Edward Newton's *The Greatest Book in the World* (1925).

A man may be a bitter atheist and still approach a Gutenberg Bible in all reverence. He will, in that case, regret somewhat that Herr Gutenberg chose a Bible to be the first masterpiece of his press, but he will venerate the Gutenberg workmanship. Won to admiration for the products of the Gutenberg press by the spectacle of this superb book, he may, if the shears fall on a sufficient quantity of coupons the first of every month, decide to go in for incunabula. Incunabula are books printed in the fifteenth century—from whatever date around the middle of that century when Johann Gutenberg began pulling proofs for his Bible to the end of the year 1500. The word is sometimes used to include books printed early in the 1500's, but this is an error. Incidentally, incunabula are the only books which are valuable on account of their age—age, that is, in the absolute sense, without qualification and without restriction of place, subject matter, or literary or historical importance. The word incunabula, by the way, is one of those formidable Latin terms which conceal an elementary metaphor. It means swaddling-clothes. An incunabulum is a book that dates back to the cradle days of printing.

Books of this period are almost without exception beautiful books—beautiful, that is, in their own right, without regard to the lack of conveniences which handicapped the early printer as a mere producer. It is true, though it is unfair to say it without explanation, that since the middle of the fifteenth century printing has progressed only in those aspects of its development which do not add to its aesthetic value. Had it remained purely an art, like the art of writing manuscript books, civilization would have remained substantially where it was. Speed and the reduced cost of production have not made for beautiful books, but they have made for a wide dissemination of knowledge. The Gutenberg Bible, printed five centuries ago—its quinquecentennial received worldwide celebration—circulated only among a select and highly reactionary literate clientele, and advanced the cause of popular education rather less than did Michelangelo's Moses or Leonardo's Mona Lisa.

It is interesting to speculate about Columbus' discovery of America. Had it preceded Gutenberg's invention instead of following it by four decades, there would have been no printing press to report it. Perhaps it would have faded into legend as many other voyages must have done.

One is apt to think of the early days of printing as a period in which only tentative if triumphant efforts were made in this significant development of human genius. Printing, however, was not only a beautiful baby, but an exceedingly healthy one. And coincident with the invention of printing appeared the tramp printer—a picturesque personage who survived until recent years, when the growth of the use of mechanical typesetting devices particularly in newspaper offices, and the standardization effected by the growth of organized labor in printshops ended his colorful career.

From Germany printing spread to Italy, where the burgeoning of the Renaissance supposedly offered a splendid field for the new craft. But, as George Parker Winship points out in *Gutenberg to Plantin* (1926), "this intellectual movement did not penetrate low enough to create a numerous book-buying public," with the result that many of the craftsmen from the Rhine Valley "worked themselves straight into bankruptcy by printing numerous editions of the literary classics." Venice quickly became the world's

AL DVS

Aldus colophon.

printing capital, and the supreme early exponent of the art in that city was Nicolaus Jenson, a Frenchman, the first printer to give his name to a font of type.

The best-known name in the annals of early Italian printing is that of Aldus. The name covers several individuals, from the first Aldus Manutius who went to Venice in 1488, to his grandson, who died in 1597. The Aldi came nearer to being popular printers than any of their predecessors had been or had attempted to be. Aldines—the products of their press, with the famous trademark of the anchor and the dolphin—do not today enjoy the vogue which once was theirs, and therefore, with some exceptions, do not command the prices they once did. But they are beautiful books, and like Elzevirs, the products of a seventeenth-century family of Dutch printers who also issued large popular editions of the classics which are now also under a temporary cloud, they will someday surely come into their own again.

Printing was twenty years old before the first book in the English language appeared. William Caxton was a man of means who took up the new craft somewhat as a hobby. It was about 1475 that he produced, at Bruges, his *Le Recueil des histoires de Troye*. The first book printed in English, therefore, was not printed in England, nor was it an original English work, but a translation.

Returning to England the following year, Caxton set up his printshop in a chapel connected with Westminster Abbey. This, by the way, is the reason why union printers in newspaper and other printshops today are organized into "chapels." The first dated book to appear at Westminster was *The Dictes or Sayengis of the Philosophres*, issued late in 1477. Some fifteen years later Caxton's shop passed, at his death, into the hands of his foreman, Wynkyn de Worde, a Fleming, whose name is worthily linked with that of the father of English printing.

HERE ends The Defence of Guenevere, and other Poems, written by William Morris; and printed by him at the Kelmscott Press, 14, Upper Mall, Hammersmith, in the County of Middlesex; & finished on the 2nd day of April, of the year 1892.
Sold by Reeves & Turner, 196, Strand, London.

The Kelmscott Press colophon.

Early books had no title pages. The title of the work, the printer's name, and the date of issue—not alone the year, but often the actual day of publication—appeared instead on the final page as a colophon. Thus the colophon of Johan Fyssher's *The Seven Penitential Psalms,* published by Wynkyn de Worde in 1509, reads:

"Here endeth the exposcycyon of the vii psalmes. Enprynted at London in the Fletestrete at the sygne of the sonne, by Wynkyn de Worde prynter unto the moost excellent pryncesse my lady the kynges grandame. In the yere of our lorde god M.CCCCC and ix and the xii daye of the moneth of Juyn."

The colophon was beautifully and effectively restored in the books produced by William Morris at the Kelmscott Press four centuries later. The masterpiece of that press, the Kelmscott Chaucer (1896), is one of the printing monuments of all time.

Of American printers, Benjamin Franklin stands first in the collector's heart. The desirability of Franklin items is, of course, enhanced by the fact that he was a great American as well as a great printer, but he was sufficiently great as a printer to hold an honored place in the history of his country even if he had never been a statesman, never helped Thomas Jefferson draft the Declaration of Independence, and never defied the lightning. His printing of Cicero's *Cato Major, or His Discourse of Old-Age* (Philadelphia, 1744) has been acclaimed as the most beautiful book printed in the Colonies. His epitaph on himself, composed many years before his death, is famous:

THE BODY

of

BENJAMIN FRANKLIN, Printer
(Like the cover of an old book,

M. T. CICERO's

CATO MAJOR,

OR HIS

DISCOURSE

OF

OLD-AGE:

With Explanatory NOTES.

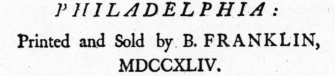

PHILADELPHIA:

Printed and Sold by B. FRANKLIN,
MDCCXLIV.

The best of Franklin's press,
Cato Major has been called the finest
example of colonial American printing.

> *Its contents torn out,*
> *And stript of its lettering and gilding),*
> *Lies here, food for worms;*
> *Yet the work itself shall not be lost,*
> *For it will (as he believed) appear once more,*
> *In a new*
> *And more beautiful edition*
> *Corrected and amended*
> *by*
> *The Author.*

Printing as an art has kept fit pace with printing as an industry ever since the days of Gutenberg. No private collector would attempt to house all the products of the notable private presses of today. The word "private" in this connection is something of a misnomer, since practically every publishing house in this country except the Government Printing Office is presumably a private enterprise. Considerable space is devoted to an attempt at a definition in Will Ransom's *Private Presses and Their Books* (1929), a manual that is essential to the collector of fine printing, and which is now available in a 1963 reissue. One definition quoted by Mr. Ransom is this: "Perhaps, in the end, the best definition of a private press is that it is an enterprise conceived, and masterfully and thoroughly carried out, by a creative artist who (whether or not he likes to cover some of his expenses by sales) does his work from a sincere conviction that he is so expressing his own personality." Mr. Ransom too generously attributes this admirably phrased explanation to Mr. Winterich, who can only say that it is not his (he wishes it were) and express the hope that due credit will one day be paid its actual originator, who is certainly a modest person, since he has been perfectly willing to allow the credit to remain with Mr. Winterich ever since Mr. Ransom's excellent bibliography was published.

It is essential to quote Mr. Ransom's own definition, which, of course, has to be broad enough to cover the scores of presses whose work is embraced in his checklists: "After all is said, the distinguishing quality of a private press is no less than a matter of spirit, indefinable except by inference. Whatever decision is made concerning the status of a press, with regard to its being private or not, must be based upon a recognition of the ideal apparent in its works, with due consideration for the human elements of its activities. Freed from the confining strictures of details, a private press may be defined as the typographic expression of a personal ideal, conceived in freedom and maintained in independence."

One of the principal exponents of fine book design in America was Bruce Rogers. He attained—deservedly—the dignity of having a book written about his work—*Bruce Rogers: Designer of Books* by Frederic Warde (1926)— which contains a checklist of two hundred books designed by Mr. Rogers and printed in various establishments, more than half of them at the Riverside Press, Cambridge. But the total reaches higher than that—Mr. Ransom's bibliography, just discussed, adds thirty-four titles (the Lerch extension), and there are subsequent additions, notably the magnificent Bible of 1935.

Of the special subject fields of book collecting—those, that is, in which authorship or design are secondary considerations, or perhaps no considerations at all—the most important is Americana. Americana means simply books about America—the term "books," in this instance, including pamphlets and broadsides. The subject is so broad that, if he expects to get anywhere within the bounds of an average lifetime, the collector will do well to confine his activities to one (or better part of one) of the many obvious divisions of the subject—the period of discovery, exploration, and settlement; the Revolution; the Civil War; the opening of the West and the development of the Pacific Coast. He may limit his efforts to a single state or group of states, and he need not select an anciently founded Eastern commonwealth to make his task pleasantly difficult.

The crowning piece of Americana is, without any question, the letter which Columbus wrote telling of "the glorious success that our Lord has given me in my voyage" and signed, simply "The Admiral." This letter is the first notice in print of the discovery of America. Unfortunately only a single copy of it exists, so that even the wealthiest collectors must do without. There is, of course, the chance that other copies may someday be discovered, for the world had to wait nearly four hundred years for the one extant. It was written to the Admiral's friend, Luis de Santangel, Commissioner of Accounts to Their Spanish Majesties, February 16, 1493, off the Canary Islands, and discovered in Spain in 1889. This copy is in the possession of the New York Public Library, and is cared for rather more tenderly than a millionaire's baby.

But Americana items need not be ancient in the absolute sense to command high figures. Mention was made earlier in this chapter of a book which, published in 1848, has sold at auction at its first and only appearance for $3,150, and it reached that figure solely on account of its age. That book is a compilation, published at San Francisco, of *Laws for the Better Government of California. . . . During the Military Occupation of the Country by the Forces of the United States.* It is the earliest book printed in English in California, and only one copy of it has ever come to light. It is as clearly and unequivocally an item of Americana as the Spanish Letter of Columbus.

Not many books concerned with the Civil War sell at an excessive premium; the literature of the period is so voluminous that a collector who devoted himself to it with intensity would soon be smothered in the vast mass of material which would pour in upon him. The same is true, in even greater degree, of the First World War. Some notable World War I libraries are already in existence, witness the impressive collection in the Hoover War Library at Stanford University. And the amount of Second World War material which Yale University, to give just one example, has already collected, is staggering.

It was Lewis Carroll's Alice who first called to public notice the uselessness of a book without pictures, and a host of collectors share her opinion. A bad artist cannot hurt a good book—much—but a great artist can dignify a mediocre book and make of it an important collector's item. The aesthetic ideal, of course, is the combination of great artist and great author.

Early picture books come high. Consider, for instance, the superb edition of Boccaccio—*De La Ruine des Nobles Hommes et Femmes*—printed at Bruges in 1476 by Colard Mansion. The book has several claims to distinction. It is the first dated book printed at Bruges, which was an important center in the early history of typography—the first book ever printed in English, as already noted, was issued there. It is the first dated book from the press of Colard Mansion, who had been Caxton's friend and associate in the Englishman's early typographical essays at Bruges. It is the first dated book with copperplate illustrations. The description of this Boccaccio in the sale catalogue of the library of the Marquess of Lothian in 1932 included this notation: "It is entirely unnecessary to insist on the importance of the above-described book, which may be said, without the slightest exaggeration, to be the most notable illustrated incunabulum ever sold by auction."

The sale of this Colard Mansion Boccaccio at New York provided one of the most dramatic moments in the history of the book auction in America or anywhere else. As it was brought out for its final public appearance before passing to other hands there was a bustle among the gallery officials, a whispering of technical confidences, a pleasurable sense of anticipation in the large audience that something out of the routine was about to happen. Then the auctioneer announced from the rostrum that a long-distance telephone call was being put through to New York from a point which he did not name, but which, it is known, was much closer to Chicago than to New York, and that the caller was going to bid on the lot. The opening bid of $25,000 was a telephoned bid, relayed from behind the scenes and from beyond the Appalachians to the floor of the auction room, and the ghostly coveter of this surpassing book carried his enthusiasm up to $40,000. He then abandoned the field to two New York booksellers, one of whom made it his a few seconds later with a bid of $45,000. One prominent bookseller who was present later complained to the gallery officials concerning this (as he regarded it) palpable piece of hocus-pocus, but they assured him that the call was genuine, as it was. The miracle of Telstar promises soon to make intercontinental auctions a commonplace.

This incident is here related not in order to discourage the intending collector of illustrated books, but rather to urge him on by impressing upon him (if he needs the impressing) the superlative status of the illustrated book in the collector's eye.

Avoiding invidious comparisons of the artistic merits of the illustrators of a century ago and those of today, one may safely say that in England of the 1820's, 1830's, and 1840's the illustrator, deservedly or not, came ahead of the author. The familiar story of the inception of *The Posthumous Papers of the Pickwick Club* provides an admirable example. Dickens was commissioned to write text to accompany sporting illustrations by Robert Seymour. Seymour shot himself before the second installment of the text was ready, and R. W. Buss was commissioned to continue the work. His etchings did not meet with the publishers' favor, so after completing only two drawings he was dismissed in favor of Phiz (Hablôt K. Browne), who carried the enterprise through. It is interesting to speculate on what would have happened had Seymour lived. Would he have insisted on holding the reins of the enterprise, and would *Pickwick* have come down to us as one of the thousand sporting books of the moment, barely known to the general reader, and known to the collector only as one obscure unit in a series that has a rather high collection value? Or would the sheer genius of Dickens have triumphed anyway, and carried the day over the inevitable protests of the artist? Needless to say, the value of *Pickwick* today is determined not by the fact that Seymour, Buss, and Phiz illustrated it, but by the fact that Dickens wrote it. Seymour and Buss, at least, shine in the reflected glory of Dickens, and such collection value as attaches to their work outside of *Pickwick* arises principally from their having had a hand in *Pickwick*. The name of Phiz, too, owes much of its glamour to the fact that he was long associated with Dickens, though he, like George Cruikshank, was great in his own right, and would have his following today even if Dickens had never been born.

Not enough attention is paid by the American collector to American illustrators, and herein lies an admirable opportunity for the lean of purse. Books illustrated by Howard Pyle and Frederic Remington have consistently been sought for many years, but not in such degree as to cause prices to skyrocket—why, by the way, is not collector attention directed to the work of the pupils of Howard Pyle? There is a growing demand, as there should be, for Peter Newell, A. B. Frost, and N. C. Wyeth. Recent years have seen the development of a collector following for several living artists, but numerous others, equally alive, are not collected but deserve to be. When we point out that many contemporary English illustrators of no higher endowments than some of our own have been eagerly collected for many years, we seek not to disparage English illustrators but rather those American collectors who blindly follow an occasionally uninspired leadership. There is room on many collectors' shelves for the finest illustrated books of the moment, English *and* American. And not necessarily of this particular moment. A two-sides-of-the-sea collection of any particular era—either a single year or a whole decade—would provide an impressive basis for the study of the art of illustrating and of the operation of influence and counterinfluence, and would be of much more than negligible interest as a social study. Two excellent guides are Theodore Bolton's *American Book Illustrators* (1938) and *Early American Book Illustrators and Wood Engravers 1670–1870,* by Sinclair Hamilton (1958).

The possibilities for the collector in the department of the illustrated book are limitless. For instance, it is not essential that he accent the illustrator—he may choose to accent the thing illustrated. While the pursuit may take him over the fence into the print collector's private patch, no harm is done thereby. Most subject collectors exhibit a broad catholicity as between prints and books—they want both. Some collectors of subject pictures, in books or out, carry their zeal for specialization far indeed. There is a collector who acquires any book within his means which contains an illustration showing a man (or a woman or a child) reading.

It may serve a purpose to go into fairly elaborate detail in the consideration of a specific instance of a planned collection in the field of the illustrated book. The collector in search of an interesting specialty the pursuit of which is not likely to involve him in fiscal catastrophe might profitably turn his attention to the first books of authors to contain their portraits. In the nature of the case these are rarely the authors' earliest books. Usually a certain amount of prestige and acceptance is implicit in the very fact of a published portrait, particularly in a book which emblazons the subject's name in the middle of its title page. And by the same token these items are not apt to be overexpensive. Inevitably there are exceptions, such as the original (1855) edition of Whitman's *Leaves of Grass*—and, unfortunately, the First Folio Shakespeare, where the problem is complicated, even for millionaires, by the fact that the portrait exists in three states. Shakespeare enjoyed the advantage (so far as his posthumous fame was concerned) of being dead at the time. Poe benefitted similarly; the first of his books to contain his likeness was the collected *Works* of 1850. So did Thoreau, whose portrait serves as the frontispiece of *Excursions* (1863). Following Stephen Crane's death, his photograph was reproduced during the same year (1900) in two books: *Whilomville Stories* and a reissue of *The Red Badge of Courage* with a biographical preface. Another exception is Phillis Wheatley's first and only book, *Poems on Various Subjects, Religious and Moral* (London, 1773; Philadelphia, 1785). Both volumes have the author's portrait as frontispieces, making her the first American poet to be so distinguished. What is further remarkable is that she was an African-born slave who became the first American poet of any renown.

Hawthorne was well advanced in bibliographic years before his portrait appeared in one of his own books. This was in the 1851 edition of *Twice-Told Tales*, which is of collector's interest on another account by reason of the eight-page preface which here appears for the first time, with its familiar allusion to the author as "for many years the obscurest man of letters in America."

Whittier's likeness first appeared in conjunction with his name on a title page in his *Poems* of 1849—"a book," declares Carroll A. Wilson, "whose neglect by collectors is to me incomprehensible, since it is not only a rather attractive book, but is also the first attempt at a complete collection, and a first edition in book form of some twenty-four of his poems." Holmes's portrait is to be found in the 1851 edition of his *Poems*, and is the only element to give the book a collector value, for it contains no text additional to that in the 1849 edition. Three of the other great New Englanders enjoyed their first visual representations in their own books in the volumes of Ticknor and Fields's Blue and Gold Series, including Lowell's *Poetical Works* (two volumes, 1858), Emerson's *Poems* (1865), and Longfellow's *Prose Works* (1857).

Mark Twain's *A Tramp Abroad* (1880) which contains, in addition to the orthodox illustrations, "three or four pictures made by the author of this book, without outside help," has a portrait frontispiece, but a real if inconsequential likeness of him had appeared on page 34 of *The Innocents Abroad* (1869).

The importance of the dust jacket as a factor in bookselling has complicated the portrait problem. A representation of Theodore Dreiser appears on the back of the jacket accompanying each volume of *An American Tragedy* (1925) and one of Ernest Hemingway on the back of the jacket of *The Sun Also Rises* (1926). And in the case of Thomas Wolfe's *Look Homeward, Angel* (1929) the first-edition dust jacket had a picture of Wolfe which later editions did not have. The collector, therefore, insists not only upon his first of *Look Homeward, Angel* having a dust jacket, but the jacket with the picture. He likewise wishes his copy of Scott Fitzgerald's *The Beautiful and Damned* (1922) to have the dust wrapper because it depicts the author and his bride.

The first portrait of Kipling to appear in one of his books was in *The Courting of Dinah Shadd* (New York, 1890)—

the collection of short stories whose publication led to the famous dispute with the Harpers, the *Athenaeum* letter of Walter Besant, William Black, and Thomas Hardy, and *The Rhyme of the Three Captains*. Hardy's portrait also first appeared in the American edition of one of his books—the paper-covered edition of *Wessex Tales* which was issued in 1888 as No. 621 in the Franklin Square Library.

One portrait of Kipling has an amusing bibliographical history. It appears on a folio broadside printing of his poem *The Female of the Species* and depicts him holding a cigarette. It is apparently a trial proof, pulled before the poem and picture appeared in *The Ladies' Home Journal* of November, 1911. Some aghast editor looking at it recalled that *The Ladies' Home Journal* was waging a violent battle against cigarette smoking just at the time, so when the magazine hit the stands Kipling was holding a cigar.

The book collecting field is the universe and every activity, every phenomenon, every idea in it. And the surface of that field has barely been scratched. In the face of such vastness and plenitude, this manual can hardly seek to attempt even a perfunctory plotting; it can only suggest, and wants only to suggest, that the intending collector follow his own bent. A few more examples of actual and unusual departments of book collecting already taken over by enthusiasts may not be out of order—and when we say taken over we do not mean occupied to the exclusion of everyone else.

There is a collector who delights in "ghost" books. Not books about ghosts (though there are collectors of those), but books written for or about others by some anonymous author. The Lilly Library's extensive Vincent Starrett collection contains a prime example. It is a "vanity book" about a departed soul, dear to her family, who shall remain anonymous here, and was subtitled "The Story of a Beautiful Life." Anonymous, of course, but with the implication that it was

The Female of the Species

A Study in Natural History: By Rudyard Kipling

When the Himalayan peasant meets the he-bear in his pride,
He shouts to scare the monster who will often turn aside;
But the she-bear thus accosted rends the peasant tooth and nail,
For the female of the species is more deadly than the male.

When Nag, the wayside cobra, hears the careless foot of man,
He will sometimes wiggle sideways and avoid it if he can;
But his mate makes no such motion where she camps beside the trail —
For the female of the species is more deadly than the male.

When the early Jesuit fathers preached to Hurons and Choctaws,
They prayed to be delivered from the vengeance of the squaws —
'Twas the women, not the warriors, turned those stark enthusiasts pale —
For the female of the species is more deadly than the male.

Man's timid heart is bursting with the things he must not say,
For the Woman that God gave him isn't his to give away;
But when hunter meets with husband, each confirms the other's tale —
The female of the species is more deadly than the male.

Man, a bear in most relations, worm and savage otherwise,
Man propounds negotiations, Man accepts the compromise;
Very rarely will he squarely push the logic of a fact
To its ultimate conclusion in unmitigated act.

Fear, or foolishness, impels him, ere he lay the wicked low,
To concede some form of trial even to his fiercest foe;
Mirth obscene diverts his anger; Doubt and Pity oft perplex
Him in dealing with an issue — to the scandal of the Sex!

But the Woman that God gave him, every fibre of her frame
Proves her launched for one sole issue, armed and engined for the same,
And to serve that single issue, lest the generations fail,
The female of the species must be deadlier than the male.

She who faces Death by torture for each life beneath her breast
May not deal in doubt or pity — must not swerve for fact or jest.
These be purely male diversions — not in these her honour dwells —
She, the Other Law we live by, is that Law and nothing else!

She can bring no more to living than the powers that make her great
As the Mother of the Infant and the Mistress of the Mate;
And when Babe and Man are lacking and she strides unclaimed to claim
Her right as femme (and baron), her equipment is the same.

She is wedded to convictions — in default of grosser ties;
Her contentions are her children, Heaven help him, who denies!
He will meet no cool discussion, but the instant, white-hot, wild
Wakened female of the species warring as for spouse and child.

Unprovoked and awful charges — even so the she-bear fights;
Speech that drips, corrodes and poisons — even so the cobra bites;
Scientific vivisection of one nerve till it is raw,
And the victim writhes in anguish — like the Jesuit with the squaw!

So it comes that Man, the coward, when he gathers to confer
With his fellow-braves in council, does not leave a place for her
Where, at war with Life and Conscience, he uplifts his erring hands
To some God of Abstract Justice — which no woman understands.

And Man knows it! Knows, moreover, that the Woman that God gave him
Must command but may not govern; shall enthrall but not enslave him.
And *She* knows, because She warns him and Her instincts never fail,
That the female of Her species is more deadly than the male!

Kipling's cigarette
was changed to a cigar.

written by the deceased's bereaved husband, the flyleaf bears the inscription, in ink:

> *I, Vincent Starrett, being at the time sound in mind but poor of pocket, undertook to compile, and did compile, this damned thing for the sum of $250, cash in hand. I now regret the circumstances exceedingly, but at the time of writing it was the circumstances that made all the difference. The innumerable clichés and the innumerable examples of bad English are the result of rewritings of my original copy. God help us all!*

There is a collector who does his collecting, as it were, in tandem. His library is constructed in pairs; he wants all the duplicated titles he can lay hands on in first edition. This business of duplicated titles is almost invariably the result of simple coincidence or of the workings of subconscious memory. One exception is Edith Wharton's *The Mother's Recompense* (1925), wherein Mrs. Wharton pays graceful tribute of acknowledgment to the memory of Grace Aguilar, who had used the title nearly a century earlier. Mrs. Wharton was not so kindly treated, however, by her own publisher. One of her finest works, *The Valley of Decision,* was issued in 1902, and forty years later Marcia Davenport's best-selling novel of the same title was issued by the same publisher without any indication of previous usage.

Rudyard Kipling's *The City of Dreadful Night* is certainly an instance of subconscious copying. Tipped to the title pages of copies of the first English edition (1891) were slips which read: "The Publishers beg to state that at the time of printing this work they had overlooked the fact that the title had been previously used for a volume of Poems by the late James Thomson (B. V.). They have, however, received the kind permission of Mr. Thomson's Publishers to use it." Thomson had died in 1882, two years after the original appearance of his own *City of Dreadful Night*.

Facing the first text page of Frank Norris' *A Man's Woman* (1900) appears the following notice signed with Norris' initials: "The following novel was completed March 22 1899, and sent to the printer in October of the same year. After the plates had been made notice was received that a play called 'A Man's Woman' had been written by Anne Crawford Flexner. As it was impossible to change the name of the novel at the time this notice was received, it has been published under its original title."

George Gissing seems to have been particularly happy in his choice of titles for his novels, for at least three of these (*Sleeping Fires, The Crown of Life,* and *The Whirlpool*) have appeared on the covers of novels written subsequently by other hands.

When titles are taken directly from quotations, familiar or unfamiliar, some duplications are bound to occur. Volney Streamer's little collection of *Book Titles from Shakespeare* records several duplications, and a compilation of titles from the Bible would doubtless record many more. Mr. Streamer's brochure, in fact, records one triplication: *Life's Fitful Fever* (from *Macbeth*), used by Edgar Fawcett, Eleanor Holmes, and Arabella M. Hopkinson.

There is a collector who specializes in the last books of authors who died by their own hands. There is a collector who seeks novels in which fictionized Presidents of the United States appear as characters (to the exclusion of novels in which actual Presidents appear, however much they may be fictionized). There is a collector who confines himself to books illustrated by their authors.

There is a collector who is assembling a library of juvenile literature by those authors who have not yet been caught up in the orbit of universal collectibility. Lewis Carroll,

Louisa M. Alcott, A. A. Milne he regards as preempted by
his betters, or at least by people better able to buy books,
and he eschews also, with what we regard as needless scorn
(but after all it is his scorn and his collection), those individual juvenile titles which already have a following:
Frances Hodgson Burnett's *Little Lord Fauntleroy* (1886),
Mary Mapes Dodge's *Hans Brinker* (1866), James Otis
Kaler's *Toby Tyler* (1881), John Townsend Trowbridge's
Cudjo's Cave (1864), and Kate Douglas Wiggin's *Rebecca
of Sunnybrook Farm* (1903). Instead he acquires so much
as he can of Palmer Cox, Kirk Munroe, Edward S. Ellis,
Elijah Kellogg, Ralph Henry Barbour, and Rossiter Johnson.
He has so far found himself facing little competition—a condition which has both its advantages and its disadvantages.
The principal advantage (and it is hardly a negligible one)
is that it consumes a considerable amount of time and
search. But this very fact augments the pleasure he takes in
the hunt. J. K. Lilly's great collection contains many great
rarities, but possibly no section of it cost so little money and
so much time and gave him more pleasure to assemble than
his Harry Castlemons. Now largely forgotten, the author
(Charles A. Fosdick) was once renowned for his boys'
books. *Frank before Vicksburg* (1865), *Frank on the Lower
Mississippi* (1867), etc., were staple fare for boys growing
up in the last decades of the past century. He so impressed
Mr. Lilly that he commissioned Jacob Blanck to do a full-
dress bibliography, *Harry Castlemon: Boys' Own Author*
(1941).

It can be set down as a collecting truism that among the
most difficult books to obtain are those for which there has
never been an active demand. This condition holds as long as
the books sell, when available, for a dollar or two. Once
demand sets them in the twenty, fifty, or thousand-dollar
class (which it occasionally does) they come out of hiding
like mice after the cat's departure. The collector thus is con-

fronted with the odd but explicable paradox of a book's becoming, so to speak, the commoner the rarer it gets.

A casual inspection of the average book-auction catalogue (and, the cynic might observe, of the average bookshop catalogue) must justify the uninitiated in the view that the book collector's hobbyhorse has never known any more exciting pasturage than the platform of a merry-go-round. Too much collecting activity merely proceeds in a not particularly vicious circle from à Becket to Zola (or occasionally to Zubly). The spectacle of a pilgrim on the threshold of bibliophily inquiring what there is left for him to collect pathetically parallels the plight of the college freshman with an English theme due in forty minutes beating the underbrush of perceptivity for something to write about.

But not all collecting is sheer uninspired copycattery. A larger independence of spirit and subject has been manifested during recent years. Consider the instance of an authority on plant pathology at Pennsylvania State College, described in the *Publishers' Weekly* by Frederick M. Hopkins, who is assembling a library on potatoes. Or the collector who is attempting to assemble a complete set of the Haldeman-Julius Little Blue Books (there are nearly 2,000 of them), which came out at a nickel each in the 1920's and were enormously successful. The New York Public Library houses in a beautiful room (where, ironically, smoking is not permitted) the enormous collection of books, manuscripts, and engravings illustrating the history of tobacco formed by George Arents, Jr.

We have before us a bookseller's catalogue listing fewer than five hundred lots, but these are divided among 164 subjects. There would be no point in listing the whole 164 here—some are already the particular passions of large groups of collectors, and others are perhaps too restricted in appeal for citation in such a generalized discussion of book collecting as here presented. But a selection from the 164 is

LITTLE BLUE BOOK NO. 1
Edited by E. Haldeman-Julius

Rubaiyat of Omar Khayyam

With a Critical Essay by
Clarence Darrow

worth offering as a modest indication of the inclusiveness of the collecting field:

Advertising, alchemy, amazons, amber, asylums, automobiles, banking, bazaars, bookkeeping, bookmarkers, boots and shoes, brewing, caricature, cattle, cavalry, ceramics, cinema, clocks, coaching, coins, color printing, cotton, cremation, cricket, cycling, earthquakes, elections, epidemics, fables, factory laws, fairs, falconry, fires, flags, funerals, furniture, gambling, games, glass, guillotine, hairdressing, horses, hospitals, hydrophobia, insurance, iron, lace, liberty of the press, literary controversies, lithography, local government, lotteries, machinery, mathematics, measures, microscopes, museums, music printing, musical instruments, names, needlework, nursery rhymes, opium, oysters, pantomimes, pawnbroking, periodicals, photography, pirates, playing cards, popular delusions, postage stamps, prisons, psychical research, public finance, publishing, riots, roads, rowing, shipping, signboards, slavery, smallpox, spoons, steam engines, stereotyping, sundials, swans, tailoring, tapestries, taxation, tea, telegraph, telephone, tin, volcanoes, weather, windmills, wine, witchcraft, women, wool, wrestling.

There has been much—doubtless too much—preachment in this chapter. Well, since it has turned itself into a sermon, let it be garnished with a text, even though the text comes at the very end. We select that text from the foreword with which the late Ralph Samuel of New York prefaced the sale catalogue of his library: "I must confess that I have never had any definite plan in collecting. If a book seemed interesting to me and promised enjoyment, it had sufficient credentials to enter my library." In our view, far from lacking "any definite plan," Mr. Samuel selected the best plan of all—the plan without which all other collecting programs, the most modest and the most ambitious alike, must be formless, purposeless, dull.

■

CHAPTER TWO

ASSOCIATION
BOOKS

■

In Eden Phillpotts's fascinating orgy of blood, *The Red Red-maynes*, the last of the three Redmayne brothers, Albert, who is a book collector, visits the house on the cliff where his brother Bendigo had made his home in order to go over the old sailor's effects after his disappearance and presumed death. Bendigo, hardy old salt that he was, would doubtless have described himself as "not much of a reader." He was, however, passionately devoted to Herman Melville's *Moby-Dick*—presumably not a first edition, since first editions meant nothing to Bendigo, and in this instance he would have been at some pains to get a copy—and spent much of his leisure reading and rereading it.

Albert Redmayne, records Mr. Phillpotts, "went through his brother's scanty library and found nothing in it of any interest to a collector." Which, by the way, is an admirable touch—anyone who has felt the slightest tug of the collecting instinct will act precisely so when set down in front of a chance bookcase. But, adds Mr. Phillpotts, "the ancient and well-thumbed copy of *Moby-Dick* he took for sentiment."

That copy of *Moby-Dick*, admittedly not in the best of

condition, would probably have been dropped in the six-penny box if Bendigo's little library had ever reached an antiquarian book dealer, or perhaps would have been thrown out altogether. But Albert Redmayne, for all his deep bibliographic knowledge, his extensive collection, his ample means for book buying, doubtless treasured it for the brief remainder of his life as one of the priceless items in his library. It was an association copy.

Everyone who owns books—including, we doubt not, some persons who cannot read—owns association copies. People who do not know the meaning of book collecting, who could not conceive the idea of a first edition, have association copies. It may be a family Bible with a faded record of births, marriages, and deaths. It may be a prize won at school. It may be the gift of a dear friend, or, like Bendigo Redmayne's copy of *Moby-Dick*, a book that has felt the touch of a loved but vanished hand. It may be a stout little volume that has deflected a bullet and saved an owner's life. It may have been a faithful companion on a far journey.

Once removed from the protection of a hand that loves them, association copies of this class are obviously of little value. But consider such association books as the following:

Shakespeare's copy of Florio's translation of Montaigne's essays, with Shakespeare's autograph on the flyleaf—one of six Shakespeare autographs that have come down to us, and the only one in a book.

The unnamed but certainly ponderous volume with which Dr. Johnson felled the bookseller.

The copy of Keats's *Lamia* which was found in Shelley's pocket after his body had been recovered from the sea.

The Yellow Book, picked up in a shabby bookstall, from which Browning created *The Ring and the Book*.

The books which Abraham Lincoln studied by the light of flaming pine knots.

Here are association books of obvious, enduring, and universal interest.

An association copy should provide of itself the proof of its association. Every antiquarian bookstore is doubtless loaded down with books that have passed through the hands of one or more famous owners, but unless at least one of those owners has left unimpeachable evidence of his ownership such books are of absolutely no association value. Someday perhaps the science of thumbprint reading may be brought into play to identify past proprietors of books, just as it is now employed to identify past proprietors of lethal weapons. Until that day, the hallmark of association identification will be the autograph.

A person is likely to write his name in a book for one of two reasons. He wants to make it plain that the book is his property, which is pretty scant protection against the average rapacious book borrower and only fair insurance against the common run of book thief. Or he wants to identify himself as the donor of the book to a friend, and writes an inscription on the flyleaf conveying title. The book may be the work of the autographer or of someone else. The commonest form of association book, and in general the most desirable, is one which is the work of the autographer and which he is bestowing on a friend. Such an inscribed book is known as a presentation copy. The more personal the inscription the more desirable the copy. Cooper presented Mrs. Banyer with "the first copy that has been issued" of his famed novel *The Spy*, making it about as fine an association copy as one is liable to come upon.

The inscription may typify any one of a multiplicity of forms, but here is one detail of life wherein form is not the principal factor to be taken into account. "A.B. from Y.Z." may tell a more compelling story than a lavish inscription occupying a full page and running over onto the next—whole

To Mrs Banyar, *from her*
Humble Servant
the
THE SPY; *Author*

A TALE OF

His first copy that
has been issued, is

THE NEUTRAL GROUND.

Respectfully

Presented

"Breathes there a man with soul so dead,
Who never to himself hath said,
This is my own, my native land.—"

BY
THE AUTHOR OF "PRECAUTION."

IN TWO VOLUMES.

VOL. I.

NEW-YORK:

WILEY & HALSTED, 3, WALL-STREET.

Wm. Grattan, Printer.

1821.

Cooper's *The Spy*: a fine association copy.

letters, indeed, indited on flyleaves are not uncommon. If Y.Z. happens to have been (or to be) among the elect of letters, his simple initialing of his donation carries more weight than a fulsome tribute paid by and to a comparative nonentity; and if A.B. also happens to stand for an important recipient—preferably a friend and familiar of Y.Z.'s—the importance of the book thus inscribed mounts geometrically.

Does the actual wording of the inscription carry weight? Other factors being equal, or nearly so, it does. A patient and painstaking collector might well devote his activities to the acquisition of a collection of association books by comparatively unimportant authors in which the inscriptions are characterized by conspicuous cleverness, or even by the lack of it. The most pleasantly memorable inscription which we have ever seen in an association copy was in a volume that reposed in the bookcase in the cabin of the captain of the Anchor liner *Tuscania*. It read, to quote it from memory: "To Captain David W. Bone from Engineer William McFee, who wishes he were a captain and had nothing to do but write."

There are authors whose inscribed books survive in an abundance that makes them almost as readily obtainable as uninscribed copies. John Galsworthy was a kindly and obliging gentleman no less than a searching and significant spectator of the human scene; apparently he never turned away anyone who thrust a book and a pen into his face and begged him write. As a result books inscribed by Galsworthy must exist in the hundreds, and the collector who wants a Galsworthy first edition (not, of course, any first edition) with the author's name on the flyleaf may have one without vast sacrifice—a consideration which, naturally, has nothing to do with Galsworthy's present or eventual place in English literature. There appeared at public sale in New York a group of four Galsworthy novels whereof the first was inscribed simply "B.B.G. with the author's love." There is considerable distinction, from whatever point of view one looks at the situation, between a book casually autographed to please a chance admirer and a book presented by the writer to his mother.

Too high a technical distinction, we feel, is placed by booksellers and auction houses (and by collectors) on the completeness or lack of it in the signing of the author's name —the distinction is carried over into the field of autograph collecting generally. A higher value is put on full name than on mere first name or initials. Why should it be? There is far more intimacy in mere first name or simple initials; the book so inscribed patently possesses a higher sentimental value. The situation is merely an instance of logic carried to such an extreme pitch that it doubles in on itself and becomes nonsense. Every inscribed book, every autograph letter, should be a law unto itself.

It would be pleasant if there were a simple rule whereby one might compute the cost variant between an inscribed and an uninscribed book. But no such yardstick is available. The instance of Galsworthy has been cited—at the other end of the spectrum is such a name as George Meredith, books inscribed by whom are excessively rare. An ordinary Galsworthy title which costs the collector, in uninscribed state, x dollars, is not likely to cost him, if carrying the author's autograph, more than $3x$ or thereabouts; a Meredith item which brings, uninscribed, x dollars may cost $50x$ or even $100x$ inscribed. We do not mean that this rule operates throughout the Galsworthy and Meredith checklists, because there are too many factors to take into account—the actual rarity of the book and the nature of the inscription among them. We do, however, wish to make it clear that the examples cited are actual catalogue entries.

Mere association interest cannot make an unimportant

book important. In fact, unimportant books, as a group, are likely to assay for a higher proportion of association interest than important books. Amateur and semiprofessional writers inevitably have to give their books away in order to get their books read—or, to be less charitable, to get their books distributed. Thus a situation frequently arises whereby inscribed copies of a book are far commoner than uninscribed, sometimes even to the extent that uninscribed copies are virtually unknown. Generally this means that the book never has been and never will be of the slightest moment to anybody, save possibly to the author, and often it becomes a supreme annoyance even to him. But this group provides an occasional exception of impressive magnitude. Edwin Arlington Robinson's *The Torrent and the Night Before* (Gardiner, Maine, 1896) is one of the most costly units of American verse of its generation. The first and only edition consisted of 312 copies, and cost the author-publisher fifty-two dollars. Many copies were sent to newspapers and magazines for review, "perhaps thirty to forty" to friends and acquaintances, and an unspecified number "to strangers who were known to me only by reputation"—among them Thomas Hardy, whose copy was sold at auction in New York at more than ten times the original cost of the whole edition. We have heard of one uninscribed copy that passed through the hands of a bookseller, but no uninscribed copy has ever appeared at auction. What occurred is obvious. The uninscribed review copies, either with or without benefit of editorial notice, were in almost every case tossed aside; most of the copies addressed to strangers must have suffered a like fate; only the friends and acquaintances (perhaps only the friends) preserved their copies. The story of *The Torrent and the Night Before* is the story of almost any comparable literary venture—save for the happy ending.

The collector of association books can begin at a dollar and graduate into the stratosphere. While it might be uselessly arbitrary for him to limit himself to the dollar, still, by permitting his price level to rise occasionally, he can assemble an entertaining library of presentation copies through which, as he progresses, a definite thread of interest will begin to be discernible. For instance, there are pleasant possibilities in personal accounts of trips abroad. Time was, particularly with the resurgence of prosperity after the post-Civil War doldrums, when the boom in European travel was reflected in a host of privately printed accounts of transatlantic journeys. These are, as a group, of varying degrees of naïveté, but the sum of them (or of so many as the collector can assemble) should provide a not unimportant delineation of the impact of Old World culture on a group of well-to-do Americans who constituted, or were at least representative of, the commercial and industrial leadership of their day. Few of these cost more than a trifle; nine-tenths of them can certainly be had each for considerably less than the price of a new novel. They are not easy to find, because most of them were the products of local presses and enjoyed largely a localized distribution. But, as has frequently been pointed out in these notes, the combination of difficulty of acquisition and low overhead should be the ideal of the modest collector.

Presentation copies of privately printed verse, most of it hopelessly mediocre, are common—and as soon as this is said a bill of exceptions must be filed in view of such a pearl-in-the-oyster as *The Torrent and the Night Before.* If the verse is somewhat less than mediocre it may be all the more desirable. There are many collectors of bad verse, and there will always be keen competition for the title of America's worst poet—or should one say America's best bad poet? Each specialist in the field has his own candidate for the honor. John Winterich's will always be Bloodgood Haviland Cutter,

whose *Long Island Farmer's Poems* of 1886 is a veritable
first folio of cacophony. David Randall's is the Hoosier farmer James B. Elmore, "The Bard of Alamo." He is remembered as the man who wrote poems on such things as
sassafras and turnip greens and railroad wrecks. One of his
most famous works is "The Monon Wreck" with its climactic
line, "Cut, oh cut my leg away!" It is just such unanimity of
differing opinion that adds zest to the pursuit and study of
Pegasuses that walk with a limp.

Sermons inscribed by their deliverers are common, and
in general not so much sought after as bad verse. (After all,
there will always be more bad prose than bad verse, and it
is not likely to be so intrinsically interesting.) Secular addresses—almost always, like sermons, in pamphlet form, and
often, again like many sermons, issued ostensibly "by request"—are about as common, and are usually characterized
by a higher degree of reader interest—higher, but not necessarily high. The collector in these two departments operates
with the advantage that his collection requires little space.
And he will certainly treasure, should he be lucky enough to
acquire a copy, Henry Lee's *A Funeral Oration on the death
of General Washington* (Philadelphia, 1800), for here Lee
says, at the top of page 19: "First in war—first in peace—and
first in the hearts of his countrymen, he was second to none
in the humble and endearing scenes of private life."

Only once, surely, has a President-to-be of the United
States put together a book which remained completely unknown (to the collecting fraternity, that is) for half a
generation. In 1946 John Fitzgerald Kennedy compiled a
tender tribute to his older brother who lost his life while
serving with our Air Force in Britain. It was called *As We
Remember Joe,* and it was printed at the University Press,
Cambridge (*not* Harvard University Press) for distribution
to family and friends. Copies were not for sale, nor was the

book copyrighted, and so (*vide* the first text page of this *Primer*) the Library of Congress never received a copy, let alone two copies. In 1963 the Lilly Library acquired a copy which the President of the United States graciously inscribed.

These are occasions where evidence other than autographic may be accepted as trustworthy indication of a former famous owner of a book. A book that has occupied a place in a famous library is worth, for that reason, a place in a humbler collection, and will distinguish it. A book that once had a place on the shelves of John Grolier, its binding bearing the benevolent inscription "Io. Grolierii et amicorum"— Jean Grolier's and his friends' "—is certain to be expensive, regardless of subject or edition or author or any other consideration. A book from the great Hoe collection will dignify any smaller collection. A book from the A. Edward Newton or Frank B. Bemis libraries gains in value from the mere fact of containing the bookplate which identifies it as having been a unit in those libraries. And, less often, the mere fact that a noted artist has designed the bookplate is enough to increase the value of a book containing that bookplate.

The ideal combination in a book from a distinguished owner's library occurs when both bookplate and signature are present. The significant exemplar is George Washington. Washington owned an extensive library—an unusually comprehensive library for his day. In many of his books, happily for posterity, he inscribed his name—invariably, we believe, on the title page. In general the title page is the last element in a book which the owner should inscribe, but everything can be forgiven a title page-inscribing owner when he happens to have been George Washington. In most of his books he inserted his bookplate—the bookplate has been many times copied, usually innocently, and impressions from the original plate are readily identifiable by the expert and even by the semiexpert. A book with Washington's signature

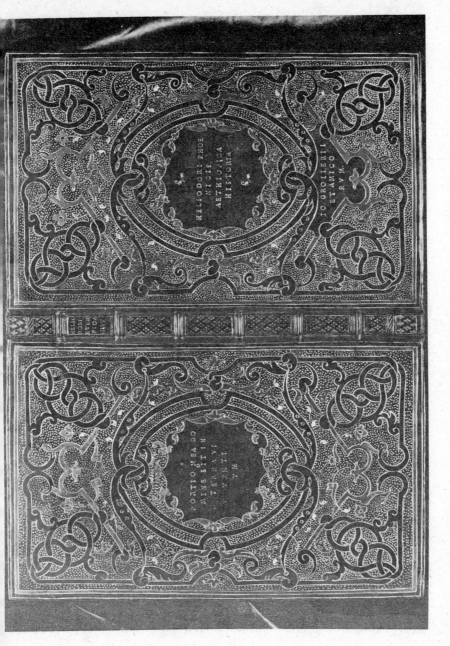

Grolier binding.

is valuable (provided, of course, the signature was actually of his fashioning) but a book with both Washington's signature *and* Washington's bookplate is much more valuable. The mere duplication of identity carries far more weight than it should. And it is of just such distinctions that the collector is occasionally able to take advantage. There are two main sorts of conventions, sound and unsound, that circumscribe virtually every human activity; the unsound conventions in book collecting are the collector's opportunity.

Books with autograph letters inserted, or "laid in," in the technical phrase, are often offered for sale. Such books are not in all strictness association copies, though they are too often thus catalogued. The buyer is actually purchasing two parcels—a book and an autograph letter. The most inclusive definition of an association book is that it is a book which has been in the hands of a famous man or woman and carries attestation of that fact. A book with an autograph letter inserted very probably has never been in the author's hands. The pursuit of autographs apart from books is no concern of the present volume, fascinating though that pursuit is, and closely allied as it is to the pastime and science of book collecting. We should be happy to have an autograph letter inserted in every book in our libraries, but we should not therefore regard every such book as an association copy. Two excellent works on autographs are Mary A. Benjamin's *Autographs: A Key to Collecting* (New York, 1946) and Charles Hamilton's *Collecting Autographs and Manuscripts* (1961).

What is true of laid-in letters is true of laid-in signatures—cutouts from the ends of letters or elsewhere. Often they are pasted in, which is undoubtedly the most sensible means of keeping them from falling out. Books containing paste-in signatures might depreciate slightly in value with the signatures removed, if only by reason of the fact that traces of paste would be likely to remain. But the presence of pasted-in signatures does not make these books association copies.

We will discuss later on the unlikeliness of parted volumes being rematched. Equally improbable is the chance of a signature cut from a letter being remarried to it. Yet such serendipities do occur. J. K. Lilly once wandered into Dr. A. S. W. Rosenbach's bookshop in Philadelphia and spotted a copy of the London, 1858, edition of Poe's *Poems* which had belonged to James T. Fields. Fields had written Sarah Helen Whitman asking for a Poe signature, and she had replied:

> *It would give me great pleasure to comply with your request had I not already parted with nearly every fragment of Mr. Poe's writing except such letters and papers as have reference to matters of a private and personal character. I sincerely wish to oblige you, but after carefully looking over these papers I find only a few detached lines here and there which I can offer you. If the enclosed postscript cut from the note dated Nov. 26, 1848, will be of any value to you it is quite at your service.*

The postscript bore the endorsement by Fields: "Given me by Mrs. Whitman," and was pasted inside the front cover of the *Poems*. Lilly purchased it on the spot, knowing he had the original letter from which Mrs. Whitman had cut away this fragment. Thus the twain met.

Occasionally one will come upon a book containing the autograph of a famous man which he used at school or college. There is a special appeal about this class of association volume. The book came into the inscriber's possession in his youth or early manhood, with fame still perhaps decades away, and with perhaps no one less aware of its approach than the inscriber himself. There is about the inscription no consciousness of autographic value; it has been put there only for strictly utilitarian purposes. "The autographs most worth having," declares Christopher Morley in

Ex Libris Carissimis, "are those that were never intended as such."

The ne plus ultra of association books is the dedication copy—the actual copy of a book bestowed by an author on the person to whom it is dedicated. The price of such an association copy is likely to be out of all proportion to the value of the book as a simple first edition, or even as an ordinary inscribed or presentation copy. The prestigious Grolier Club of New York reached deep into its members' private collections in the spring of 1965 and came up with a remarkable show displaying dedication copies only. One of the most amusing inscriptions appeared on the flyleaf of a book in which a mother recounted the rearing of her seven children: "To my husband without whose collaboration this volume would not exist."

Books are sometimes issued in limited and signed editions which are often desirable as first editions, though in most cases the regular edition is likely to be printed first, and to be the authentic first edition. Are such books association copies? True, they possess the qualifications for an association copy as we have defined it; namely, a book which has been in the hands of a famous man or woman, usually the author, and contains clear proof of that fact. But most collectors place them in a category of their own. They can hardly be called association copies save in the most matter-of-fact and literal sense of the term; they are not necessarily first editions; they are neither fish, flesh, fowl, nor good red herring. They are just what they are called—units of a "limited and signed" edition. The collector has to have them, but often he wishes there were a way out. For our part, we should prefer a copy of the ordinary first edition of a book, with the author's inscription, to a copy of the limited and signed edition of the same book. There is nothing exclusive about a book issued in an edition of 750 copies—or at least there is nothing exclusive about it until the 751st customer happens along.

Sometimes the author will simply autograph a leaf which is later tipped into the book. In 1906 Mark Twain signed a quantity of leaves for this purpose, not all of which were used. The cache was discovered in 1922, twelve years after his death, and the leaves were used to fatten up a set of his works which was about to be published. No one would have laughed more heartily over this "autographed" edition than Mark himself.

The lean years that followed the depression themselves imposed a severe limitation on the limited edition industry. No one rejoiced thereat more than the rare bookseller, unless possibly the collector. In the gay years of financial irresponsibility preceding the slump the limited-edition business was carried to such heights (or depths) that the bookseller developed into its most enthusiastic opponent. Frequently he was the victim of such a procedure as this:

A new book of verse by Horace Epode, a collected poet, would be announced by his publishers, to appear, in addition to the "regular" edition, in a limited signed edition of ninety copies. Mr. A, bookseller, investigates his files and finds the names of ten Epode collectors. He duly warns them of the imminence of the Epode limited. Eight of the ten order copies, and Mr. A accordingly places an order for eight Epode limiteds with the publishers. The book is issued —and Mr. A receives four copies. The limited edition, it appears, was heavily oversubscribed, and it became necessary to prorate copies on a 50 percent basis.

Mr. A's task is now relatively simple. All he has to do is to decide which half of his eight clamorous customers are to be allotted the four copies. Then he has to write a letter to each of the luckless quartette and explain why he cannot accommodate them. Then he has to sit back and wait for the explosion. Sometimes there is no explosion—he just never hears from those four customers again. Sometimes he hears once—a parting shot telling him, at vitriolic length and with abundant biological and genealogical detail, exactly what the customer thinks of him.

This is what was once likely to happen, and what usually did happen, when limitation has been severely restricted. When the restriction rose from a supposititious ninety to, say, five hundred or a thousand it became no restriction at all, and instead of having four books for eight customers Mr. A might have eight books for four customers.

The times themselves have operated in the adjustment of the difficulty. In recent years most limiteds have been restricted in size to the number of orders received by a specified date, with the result that the bookseller knows precisely where he stands. It is a sensible modification, and should be continued, as it probably will be.

An author's own copy of his own book is an attractive association copy. But there always exists the possibility—nay, the likelihood—that an author is apt to own more than one copy of his own book. The mere presence of the signature of an author on the flyleaf of a book written by him is not, of course, prima facie evidence that that particular copy was once in his possession. No dealer and no auction house will describe an inscribed book as the author's own copy unless there is no question that the book actually is that.

The sentimental value of more than one personality may be bound up in an association copy. An author may give a book to a man as famous as, or more famous than, himself. But a book presented by a famous author to a person not so famous, or not famous at all, is worth very much more than a book given by an unknown to a great man—unless the great man has taken the pains to annotate the volume, or merely to inscribe his name in it as proof of his ownership of it. When Joseph Conrad's library was dispersed after his death, scores of volumes came on the market which bore inscriptions bestowing them on Conrad. Most of them sold for little more than the price of a new novel. The few in which Conrad had placed his name (in some cases he inked his monogram on the cloth cover) were quoted at considerably higher figures.

As between a book inscribed "A from B with all good wishes" and a book inscribed, in the same hand, "A from B Nov 16 23," the collector will prefer the latter. A dated inscription, under ordinary circumstances, is more significant than an undated. The dated inscription often lends the book an important bibliographic value. This is particularly true of a book published late in the year—1874, for example, and carrying the date 1875 on the title—which the author has bestowed as a Christmas gift in 1874. A few James Whitcomb Riley titles were postdated by the publishers by as much as three months—a fact that will be as readily determinable a thousand years hence as it is today if a fraction of the multitude of signed Riley books survives.

The search for association books has reached its apotheosis in recent years with several efforts actually to reconstruct the libraries of famous men, from Thomas Jefferson's on down. Sometimes a famous library is passed on intact. Harvard has Thomas Wolfe's; Princeton, F. Scott Fitzgerald's; Indiana, Upton Sinclair's; and it has been reported that the library that will honor President John F. Kennedy's memory will contain Ernest Hemingway's. A rather different example of an association collection is to be found at the Folger Library in Washington, where, among other treasures, are assembled a large group of the copies of Shakespeare owned by famous men.

■

CHAPTER THREE

WHAT MAKES A RARE BOOK RARE?

■

Auction and dealers' catalogues are likely to classify a book as scarce, rare, very rare, exceedingly rare, or excessively rare. From excessively rare it is no long step to such a clear-cut mathematical delimitation as "one of six known copies" or "only one other copy known." There is one rarer class still: books which exist in only a single copy. And, to stretch the definition of rare to the breaking point, there are books—or were books—which are known to have existed at one time but of which not a single copy is extant. Knowledge of their former existence may persist through a contemporary reference or through the chance preservation of a single page, or even part of a page, used, perhaps, to reinforce the backbone of a book printed at a later date.

Now none of the terms listed above professes to estimate

with anything like accuracy the number of copies of a given book that are still in existence. It would be highly convenient if "scarce" meant that from two hundred to three hundred copies of a certain title were extant, "rare" from one hundred to two hundred, and so on. But it is never possible to tell. Even when an edition is "strictly limited to seven hundred and fifty numbered copies" one cannot be sure, though if such a notice bears the imprint of a reputable publisher the buyer has little cause for concern. But not all publishers, unfortunately, are reputable, so that the owner of No. 237 of a "limited edition" of a specified number of copies of a book by a specified author may someday disconcertingly collide with a fellow-worshipper at the same shrine who owns another No. 237. It was the habit of the late Thomas J. Wise merely to print on any of his numerous privately issued pamphlets, some fakes and some genuine: "This is one of five (or thirty) copies." None were numbered, and there is absolutely no way of ascertaining if more were done or not, though at the rate certain of the titles show up he certainly must have printed them by the scores at least.

Here is another possibility: A collector once acquired a short unpublished manuscript of a famous living author. Forthwith he sent a typewritten copy of it to a printer with an order for three printed copies in pamphlet form. The order was duly executed and the three copies—"of excessive rarity"—were stowed away in a safe. It was the plan of the owner of the manuscript and of the three pamphlets to hold the latter against the day of his need, on the theory that, the reputation of the author increasing meanwhile, and his collection value along with it, the pamphlets would grow more valuable with the passage of years—a wholly legitimate assumption.

Imagine his dismay, therefore, to read one day that a copy of one of his carefully hoarded pamphlets had been sold at auction at a high figure. Investigation showed that the three copies deposited in the safe were still exactly where they had been put. The inevitable conclusion was that the printer, having some knowledge of book collecting, and quite aware of what was in the manuscript owner's mind, had struck off at least one extra copy on his own account. Had he struck off more than one? Would he from time to time let a copy filter through to the auction rooms? Would he—horrible thought!— die, and would an inventory of his estate disclose a whole carload of the pamphlets, with a consequent hopeless break in market value? Nightmares like this doubtless ruined the sleep of the owner of the manuscript for many nights, and may be ruining it still. For there is no way under the sun in which he can determine the actual number of copies of his pamphlet in existence.

This is the only instance we know of where this form of deviltry has been laid at an unscrupulous printer's door. But it is always possible that, with no ethical question involved, several copies of a hitherto excessively rare book will come to light. Suppose the printer of Poe's *Tamerlane* (Boston, 1827) happened one hundred years ago to store away a bundle of the books against future orders which never came. Suppose there were fifty *Tamerlanes* in that bundle, and that it should suddenly be discovered by someone who knew of their value. What would happen to the *Tamerlane* market? To assume that such a bundle exists is, of course, highly fantastic, and to assume that it would be discovered by a book fancier, rather than by a janitor who would dump the whole business into a trash pit, is more fantastic still—but not beyond the broad bounds of possibility.

There is a great deal of mystery about *Tamerlane*, the so-called "Black Tulip" of American literature. Absolutely nothing is known about its printing, or printer (who was a youth of eighteen named Calvin F. S. Thomas who is not known to have printed any other book). It was a juvenile effort if ever there was one. The Preface reads: "The greater part of the Poems which compose this little volume, were written in the year 1821–2, when the author had not completed his fourteenth year. They were of course not intended for publication; why they are now published concerns no one but himself." This is all we know about the book except for Poe's only other reference to it in his second volume, *Al Aaraaf, Tamerlane and Minor Poems* (Baltimore, 1829), which contains the note to *Tamerlane:* "Advertisement. This poem was printed for publication in Boston, in the year 1827, but suppressed through circumstances of a private nature." Perhaps there *is* a "remainder" somewhere.

A real-life approximation of this hypothetical situation occurred in the instance of Stephen Crane's *Maggie: A Girl of the Streets,* the erroneously designated "privately printed" edition of 1893. Crane, unable to find a publisher for his maiden offering, had it printed at his own expense, and distributed through the recognized channels for the dissemination of paperbound books. Not quite every copy was returned to the distributors; Crane himself gave away a few. The book became excessively rare, and the resurgence of Crane's fame in the 1920's lent the item a collector luster that was not at all diminished by the sheer unavailability of the book.

The John Quinn copy, sold at auction at the end of 1923, brought $115 despite the fact that it was hardly in the freshest of condition. Early in 1925 the same copy sold for $130. Thereafter, although Crane's name appeared regularly in successive auction seasons, no copy of the 1893 *Maggie* reached the rostrum until March, 1930, when a signed presentation copy, the first to appear at public sale, brought the amazing price of $3,700, still the record price for the book.

Behind that figure was an accumulated demand, a con-

centrated eagerness to own an 1893 *Maggie,* that had perforce been bottled up for five years. *Maggie,* despite her
humble origin, had attained more than respectability—she
was among the elect of bibliophilic aristocracy.

Two months later—May, 1930—a second *Maggie* visited
the auction room, uninscribed, and fetched $2,100. It was
the property of Mrs. Florence Coghlan, a niece of Crane.

The result of these previously unimagined figures was that
an intensive search for *Maggies* was undertaken throughout
the book trade. During the 1930–1931 season three copies
reached the block—they sold, respectively, for $500, $775,
and $1,125, the last inscribed. Four copies appeared in the
1931–1932 season. They sold, in the order of their appearance, for $550, $230, $85, and $90.

Only the first of these four was in good collector condition.
But a consideration that lay deeper than condition, important as that consideration itself is, was responsible for the
descending curve. The fear had gripped the book trade, and
the world of collectors as well, that a vast trove of *Maggies*
had been unearthed and was being doled out too swiftly for
the public to digest them. The rumors became quite definite,
as rumors have a way of becoming. These fresh *Maggies,*
said the rumors, had been found in a soapbox—even a piano
box—at such-and-such a place in New Jersey, in such a corner of an old stable, and there were so-and-so many copies.
The figure was always specific, but the specificness was never
the same.

Only one *Maggie* appeared the following season (1932–
1933). A rebacked presentation copy, it brought $400. The
following season recorded the vending of only a single copy
—a presentation that fetched $320. Two seasons earlier the
same copy had sold for $230. At the close of 1934 another
presentation copy, rebound in cloth, brought $210. It looked
as if *Maggie*'s good name might yet be preserved.

The panic began to abate. The tide of *Maggies* was definitely slackening. Perhaps the recently discovered copies had been contained in a shoebox rather than a piano box. Reasonable dealers and collectors began to consider the fact that, after all, these presentation copies could hardly have come out of the box; they had obviously been brought to light from as many separate recesses as a result of the $3,700 figure of March, 1930. Equally obviously, there was in all probability some common source whence had appeared some of the uninscribed copies which had also been brought out by the March, 1930, record.

Then, in April, 1935, the full story came out. A fine copy of *Maggie* was offered for sale at auction in New York, and to the usual catalogue description of the lot offered was appended this explanation:

In view of the uncertainty that exists in the minds of collectors and dealers regarding a so-called "large number" of copies that are supposed to have been found, we think it advisable to make the following statement:

From March 11, 1930, to December 5, 1934, eleven copies of this work appeared at public sale in America, three of which were presentation copies; some of the volumes were in very poor condition. Nine of the eleven were sold in these galleries, the first (a presentation copy) on March 11, 1930, and the last (also a presentation copy) on December 5, 1934. Only two, however, of the nine that we have sold were the property of the owner of the present copy, Mrs. Florence Crane Coghlan.

When Mr. Coghlan came to the Galleries to negotiate the sale of the present copy, we gave it as our opinion that it would be unwise to offer it for sale unless a definite statement was made in the catalogue regarding the exact number of copies still held by him and his wife.

We are informed that they still hold eleven copies and

*that the present copy is one of the finest, being practically
as fresh as on the day it left the printers' hand. The
majority of the others are in more or less worn condition,
some with the wrappers slightly chipped, and others torn,
lightly stained, or with other slight defects.*

*An arrangement has been made with Mr. and Mrs.
Coghlan whereby these eleven copies are to be sold in these
Galleries at the rate of two copies each season hereafter
until the entire number has been distributed.*

In view of the unusual circumstances and the carrying
power of the original rumor, the officials of the Galleries
asked Mrs. Coghlan to explain the situation in a detailed
statement given over her name. This statement, one of the
most unusual in the history of book collecting, merits reproduction here for its fullness and detail:

*After the death of my father, Stephen Crane's brother
William, in California several years ago, two copies of
Maggie were sent to my sister Agnes and me by the estate.
Not knowing the value, but suspecting that they would
bring a few dollars at least, I took them to the Anderson
Galleries, where I was congratulated on the possession of
these books and they were put up at auction. The result
is book history.*

*Like everyone else, who had ever seen or heard of
Maggie, I racked my brains to remember any more possible
copies in the family library. When our home in Brooklyn
was broken up, most of our possessions were stored on
my grandfather's farm, and I mentally repacked the books
which had been sent there.*

*As far back as I could remember there had always been a
small pile of paper-bound Maggies in our storage room,
but when I spoke of this to my mother she said she didn't
believe there were any left, as my two eldest sisters had
burned them, believing they were "not nice."*

*However we took a chance and went to the farm, where
our books had been stored in a wagon house for twenty
years, and we found the books which the American Art
Association Anderson Galleries Inc. are now handling. To
my knowledge these are the only first edition Maggies in
our branch of the family.*

As a result of the restoration of public confidence in
Maggie which followed publication of this statement, the
first Coghlan copy brought $700. A number of copies have
appeared subsequently in varying states of condition, and
the last one sold at auction, in 1949, brought $425. *Maggie*
has again become a very scarce book.

These three instances—the disreputable "limited edition"
publisher, the dishonest printer, the chance of a sudden trove
of mislaid copies—are all extreme ones, but they will, we
think, give some indication of the hopelessness of trying to
gauge with anything approaching accuracy the number of
copies of a given book in a given edition which may be in
existence.

Now it is quite possible that an edition of a book may be
represented by but a single copy, and the book, relatively
speaking, not be "excessively rare" for the reason that nobody
wants it. It is also possible that a book may exist in five
hundred copies and still command a forbidding premium—
if, say, two thousand collectors want copies. It has been
said of the First Folio of Shakespeare's plays (1623) that it
is not, in all literalness, a scarce book, since a large number
of copies, several of them imperfect, are known to exist, and
that its high price is a real tribute to its importance in the
annals of English letters and to the esteem in which Shakespeare is held. This is doubtless in some measure true, but
only in some measure, because a man who is bidding on a
First Folio by five-hundred-dollar jumps is not concerned

primarily with establishing a benefit fund for the heirs of the Shakespeare estate. The reason, above all others, why a First Folio brings about as much as a substantial country estate within commuting distance of New York City is that enough men and women want a copy, and can afford to pay well for it, to keep the figure high. How many First Folios would have to be in existence to lower the price appreciably is a question no one can answer. Probably the extra copies would soon be absorbed by collectors who could afford not x but $x/3$ dollars, and before many seasons the figure would be back at the higher amount, or above it. The really great Hogan-Rosebery copy sold at auction in New York in the Frank J. Hogan sale for $50,000.

Books are rare for a number of reasons. A book can become rare at the source if only a few copies are printed. A classic example is provided by Robert Frost. Of his first book, *Twilight*, he has recorded: "I had two copies printed and bound by a job printer in Lawrence, Mass., in 1894 probably out of pride in what Bliss Carman and Maurice Thompson had said about the poem in it called 'My Butterfly.' One copy I kept for myself and afterwards destroyed. The other I gave away to a girl in St. Lawrence University." It was the girl he later married. This surviving copy, which sold at auction in New York in 1951 for $3,500 (the highest price ever paid for a book by a living American author), is now in the famous Waller Barrett collection of American literature at the Alderman Library, University of Virginia. This figure nowhere approaches the record price paid, while he was living, in 1927, of $14,000 for Rudyard Kipling's famous rarity *The Smith Administration*.

The authorship of Elinor Wylie's first book, *Incidental Numbers* (London, 1912), only sixty copies printed, was a closely guarded secret. The copy in the Louis Untermeyer collection of poetry in Indiana's Lilly Library is inscribed:

"To my dear and honoured friend Louis Untermeyer who retains that title of respect and affection only so long as he faithfully preserves the strict Anonymity of The Author."

A book that is rare, so to speak, at birth, is likely to be a proof copy, or one struck off for the author's personal use, or to hold copyright, or for the deliberate purpose of creating a market. Thus among the very rarest (though not the most expensive) of all Anthony Trollope's works are four small pamphlets, each from thirty-two to forty-four pages, printed in large type sometime in the 1860's. They are *The Civil Service as a Profession, The Present Condition of the Northern States of the American Union, Higher Education of Women,* and *On English Prose Fiction as a Rational Amusement.*

These were lectures Trollope delivered, and for his personal use he had a very few copies printed in large type to read from while on the platform. He was in the habit of delivering the same lecture in different places, and on occasion he may have handed copies to the reporters present to help them in their reviews. At any rate no copies were ever put on the market for public sale, and because of the very small number originally printed, they are now rather rare. But they are of main interest to the ardent Trollopian who wants "the master" complete. The ordinary collector and reader of Trollope, who desires firsts of the Barchester or Parliamentary series only, will pass them by—but that ardent collector Morris L. Parrish thought so highly of them, and felt so keenly for collectors who could not possess the originals, that he reprinted them in 1938 in editions of 150 copies each which in their turn have become difficult to acquire.

Almost any rare-book dealer can show you a cluster of yellow-wrapped pamphlets containing sometimes no more than a single short poem—first American editions of Rudyard Kipling, issued by his American publishers to secure American copyright. These pamphlets become collectible at the source. Since they travel in a virtually direct route from publisher to collector, they have little chance to get lost, and the number of them is not likely to diminish unless several fine libraries go up in flame or down in flood.

Production costs are today so high that no publisher would think of printing half a dozen copies of a book the size of the average novel and then destroying the plates on the theory that the books might someday attain a high collection value. The average first edition of a book is likely to be at least twenty-five hundred copies, more likely five thousand. During the printing of these thousands some slight change may be made whereby a skilled or lucky investigator may later be able to establish a priority in printing between different copies of the same edition—a business to be discussed at length in a later chapter. Perhaps, too, not all of the thousands are bound, and do not become books in the mercantile sense. Then again books may be common in one place or at one time and be desperately rare in another place and time. Consider the case of an edition of John Steinbeck's *The Moon Is Down,* translated into French as *Nuit sans Lune.* Scores of thousands of copies in a miniature edition designed as propaganda were dropped over occupied territories in 1942 by the Royal Air Force. It may even now (though we doubt it) be a common book in Flanders Fields, but it is definitely uncommon in America; and a copy in the Hogan sale brought $65.

Let us trace the dispersion of a hypothetical edition of a hypothetical book by a hypothetical author. Homer Jones sends the manuscript of a book of verse, *Thoughts,* to a publisher. Not, perhaps, to the surprise of Homer Jones, but greatly to the surprise of his friends, the manuscript is accepted. The publisher sees in *Thoughts* a depth of emotion and a felicity of phrase that cause him to believe he is doing a service to literature, and a good stroke of business for the firm, in bringing out the book. He realizes, however, that books of verse do not customarily become best sellers—that not every poetical pickup is another *Spoon River Anthology* —so he prints only a small edition of *Thoughts,* say five hundred copies.

Possibly the publisher is able to convince some English publishing firm that *Thoughts* is an original and distinguished production. The English house agrees to take two hundred of the five hundred copies printed. These two hundred copies, printed but probably not bound in America, will carry the imprint of the English publisher, and will therefore become exemplars of the first English edition. As such they are never likely to command much of a premium as collector's items, for Mr. Jones is an American, and collectors will prefer the American imprint.

Three hundred copies are left to be disposed of in the American market. In time two hundred of these reach the hands of as many booksellers as are sporting enough to risk their good money in verse. Possibly fifty copies find their way into public libraries, where, owing to the wear and tear —particularly the tear—to which a library book is ceaselessly subject, they soon become unfit for consideration by the collector (to say nothing of the fact that they contain the library stamp, are probably rebound in the library's own distinctive binding, and are the library's property in perpetuity, which means, in practice, until they fall apart).

Fifty copies are left on the publisher's hands. *Thoughts* fails to arouse great enthusiasm in the book-buying public, and there are no reorders. So within a few months the publisher disposes of the fifty copies as "remainders," receiving for them only a fraction of the cost of manufacture. The fifty copies—brand new, dust wrapper and all—find their way to the bins of the antiquarian book dealers, and are offered to an uneager world at perhaps twenty-five cents each. Only a copy or two may be visible, but the rest are safely stowed away in a storeroom, and if you bought the only copy in sight another would replace it as soon as you had left.

Somehow, in the course of time (many years, perhaps), 250 copies of *Thoughts* gravitate to 250 bookshelves in 250 homes. In the process, or after it, possibly fifty copies may be destroyed. The estimate may be too large or too small, but it will serve. For a book is at best a fragile thing, beset by enemies real or potential throughout the course of its physical life—fire, water, dust, children.

Man is a nomadic animal, especially in these gasoline days, and among the impedimenta which he is most ready to dispense with are books. One hundred of our 250 families move; a telephone brings the secondhand book dealer (or the secondhand furniture dealer, who is usually willing to remove books out of the goodness of his heart but sets small store by them), and one hundred copies of *Thoughts* are back on the market. Perhaps fifty of them are so much the worse for wear that they are thrown away as unusable.

There on the shelves of fifty antiquarian dealers the fifty copies may repose forever, but it is not likely. Every book seems to get sold in some way to somebody—and no commodity is sold so many times as a book. Casual browsers hunt down the fifty, attracted by the binding, the title, the portrait of the agreeably sad-appearing Mr. Jones that serves as frontispiece, the fact that Mamie liked that so it must be good, the fact that Mamie didn't like it so it must be good, the fact that Mr. Jones has since produced a remarkable first novel, or an equally remarkable—and, let us hope for Mr. Jones's sake, far more successful—first play.

In fact, Mr. Jones may have become so famous in the interval that *Thoughts* will have attained a collection value. In that case the antiquarian bookseller, if he knows his business, will dispose of any copies that come his way to a rare-book dealer, who will in turn sell them to collectors. If the antiquarian dealer does not know his business, it is likely that a scout, which is trade slang for the browser who knows books and book values and preys on the innocent antiquarian dealer (it is the dealer's own fault if he is innocent), will someday ferret it out, buy it for fifteen cents, and either sell it to a rare-book dealer at a handsome profit or add it to his own collection.

But we are not all nomads. One hundred owners of *Thoughts* (fifty copies, remember, have vanished from the earth) will not move, and the one hundred copies which they own may remain on their shelves for a lifetime—a human lifetime, not the longer lifetime of a book that is properly housed and tended. Eventually—it may take several generations—all of these hundred copies are almost certain to come on the market again. Meanwhile the wastage goes on; moth and rust continue to corrupt; copies of *Thoughts* are carried abroad and do not come home—rare books born in England and America have been found as far away as South America and China, and secondhand books in English of course dot the trail of the tourist in Europe.

At the end of fifty years how many copies of the first edition of *Thoughts* survive? It is impossible—hence all the more exciting—to attempt an estimate. Unless the edition were fairly herded into destruction, probably a third of the original edition should be extant. And unless the edition has enjoyed a peculiarly cloistered existence, not over two-thirds should be extant. That is, between one and two hundred copies ought to be in existence, though not necessarily available to the collector. Of other editions—the book may have been reprinted a hundred times—thousands of copies may remain to assist the author's immortality. But the collector will have no truck with these.

What will be the eventual fate of the one to two hundred

copies of the first edition? One of three things—or two of three or even all three of three—will happen to them:

They will continue to recur for sale, passing through the hands of successive owners.

They will become the property of libraries, museums, universities, or other institutions enjoying perpetual existence, and so disappear forever from the market.

They will be destroyed.

Here are some case histories:

William Carlos Williams financed his first privately printed *Poems* (Rutherford, New Jersey, 1909) and sold four copies at twenty-five cents each. A copy was recently offered for sale at $1,700. Eleven are known, but only two are of the first issue, before numerous errors were corrected. This makes the book runner-up to Frost's *Twilight* in the twentieth-century American poetry rarity sweepstakes. Most of the edition was destroyed when the henhouse in which the printer stored it was burned. Robinson Jeffers' bibliographer relates that his first book, *Flagons and Apples* (Los Angeles, 1912), "was published entirely at the author's expense in an edition of 500 copies at $1. . . . Of the 500 copies printed, R. J. left 480 with the printer; of the 20 copies he took he gave away three or four and burned the rest. The printer subsequently sold the 480 remaining copies to a secondhand bookstore for 20 cents a copy." *In Reckless Ecstasy* (Galesburg, Illinois, 1904), "By Charles A. Sandburg," was printed because a friend had a printing press in his cellar and wanted to use it. Fewer than ten copies have survived. Archibald MacLeish's Yale *Class Poem* (New Haven, 1915), a four-page leaflet, precedes his first published book by two years, and is difficult to come by, though its author has remarked that after its reading at graduation, the ground was littered with it as people tossed their copies away and went home.

A similar fate was in store for an A. E. Housman production. Housman had a passion for accuracy, which is a good passion to have. When an unwanted comma appeared in one of his verses, he wrote his publishers that he "knew the filthy beasts of printers would do something" and he only wondered what it would be. It is ironical that errors and misprints would pursue this great precisionist even to his grave. The *Times* of London in its obituary gave his age as seventy-six instead of seventy-seven. But worse was to come. Housman left a poem "For My Funeral" which was issued in an edition of three hundred copies which were distributed to mourners at the 1936 services, most of whom probably left their copies in their seats. The printers, the august Cambridge University Press, set "Ecclesiasticus" where Housman had written "Ecclesiastes." The press made amends by running off a corrected reprint of one hundred copies, thus giving the compleat collector the job of acquiring both versions (the second *should* be, but may not be, three times rarer).

There are certainly thousands of sought-for books—books worth from five dollars to a thousand and more—on the shelves and in the attics of American homes in which no one has the slightest conception of their value. The attempt to hunt them out, however, would not be worth the effort involved, for to right and to left and above and below those thousands are tens of millions of books of no slightest collection value at all.

If a book is suppressed, for whatever reason, it is likely to command an immediate premium which it may not deserve. For it may be worth collecting only for the adventitious reason of suppression, and to suppress a book is the poorest way in the world to try to exterminate it; the very fact of suppression tends to make the possessor of a suppressed book bestow more care upon it than he otherwise would. To most people suppression connotes merely smut, but a book may be suppressed because the author is displeased with its

mechanical appearance, because he regards it as an imma-
ture or ill-considered work not likely to enhance his reputation, because of a copyright dispute, because it is pirated,
because it contains libelous statements. In few of these instances is the suppression heralded with the fanfare of trumpets. Any suppression attended with hullabaloos and banners
may be merely a device of salesmanship.

When a book is issued in a limited, or limited and signed,
edition it is not likely that the original number will ever
diminish appreciably. The fact of limitation makes an immediate appeal to the collector as distinguished from the
reader—to the person who will take good care that no harm
comes to it; who may, indeed, buy another copy of an ordinary edition to read. The appeal of the limited edition is
usually directly to the collecting instinct—we are not considering, of course, the so-called limited editions of elaborate
superbound sets of whatnot and whonot that appeal to the
lust for the pompously exclusive. And the price of a book
issued in a limited edition is usually sufficient to make the
buyer treasure his purchase carefully, and not to leave it
where water will drip on it or well-meaning friends borrow it.

Among books, as among living creatures, the physically
fittest survive. Your clothbound dictionary is always close by
for you to consult—but can you lay hands immediately on a
desired railroad timetable? There are hundreds of valuable
books which are as physically flimsy as—even much flimsier
than—the average timetable. Both at Davos Platz in Switzerland and while he was in California, Stevenson toyed with a
tiny printing press, and even made little woodcuts for it. The
products of these presses, some of them four-page leaflets
half the size of this page, are today worth many times their
weight in gold. Not many of each issue were printed, and
they were so fragile that probably most of them have been
destroyed.

Consider, too, the Victorian novels which were issued in parts. Dickens' first and last books so first appeared. These parts were paperbound monthly publications, smaller in size and much less substantial in format than the average cheap magazine of today. It is easy to see that these parts would vanish by the thousand, which is why a perfect *Pickwick,* "the original twenty parts in nineteen"—for one part was a double number—is so rarely met with and so dearly priced when it is met with. When Dickens was writing *Pickwick* he was nobody—or remained nobody until Sam Weller was born. But when *Edwin Drood* appeared, thirty-four years later, Dickens was not only immensely popular, but had attained a collection value, so that an *Edwin Drood* of 1870 in the original parts—only six—is today worth only a tiny fraction of what *Pickwick* would cost. Dickens' *Great Expectations* (1861), by the way, was not published in parts, but in the three-decker format of the mid-Victorian era. The edition was small, and was taken up in virtual entirety by circulating libraries, which explains why a *Great Expectations* in good condition is today worth several hundred dollars.

When books are published in parts or in two or more volumes, it is obviously a simple matter to ruin them from the collector's standpoint by losing one of the parts or one of the volumes. The odd volume is the plague of the collector. In his hands are Volume I and Volume III of such a rarity as *Great Expectations*. Where is Volume II? Possibly in Kamchatka or Herzegovina. Unfortunately, if he looks at the matter from a mercenary point of view, it does not follow that, because *Great Expectations* entire is worth, say, $500, Volumes I and III together are worth $333.33.

To the collector, and even more to the bookseller, a broken set is cause for more acute distress than is a broken leg. The leg has a chance to mend, the set none at all. Every bookman has heard marvelous stories of sets being matched by a succession of coincidences that would shame the wood-pulp school of fiction—of a Volume One in Bangor and a Volume Two in Butte which contrive to reunite. But the stories are never confirmable.

There are two stories of rejoined sets which have for years been going the rounds of the rare-book trade and which are worth retailing here whether or no the reader is ready to accept them as gospel.

In Story One, a bookman exploring the shops on Boston's Cornhill upsets a pile of books doing service as a doorstop. Stooping to rearrange the pile, he notes that one unit is Volume One of *The Federalist* (New York, 1788), and that it bears the signature of Daniel Webster on the title page. Odd volume though it is, he buys it for the small sum demanded— perhaps Webster owned only Volume One (the pair were published at different times). A year or two later, while on a visit to Chicago, the same bookman visits an antiquarian bookstore on the edge of the Loop. Here, too, oddly enough, a refractory door is held in place by a pile of books. Again his not so luckless foot upsets the pile, again his courteous hand restores it, again his alert eye notes the names of the books—and among them, inevitably, is Volume Two of *The Federalist* with Daniel Webster's signature on the title page.

In Story Two, a book scout bound for New York City from upper New York State pauses in Albany to investigate the local situation. He finds a copy of Volume One of *Peter Parley's Universal History on the Basis of Geography for the Use of Families* (Boston, 1837), the importance of which consists in the fact that Nathaniel Hawthorne and his sister compiled it as a piece of hackwork for S. G. Goodrich. It is a scarce and valuable book. The scout acquires it for a small sum on account of its orphaned state, noting carelessly that the flyleaf bears the name of an ancient owner—Jason Peebles, let us say. The scout continues New York-ward, and, loth to miss any opportunity, stops in Poughkeepsie,

where, in a secondhand furniture store, he finds a Volume
Two of *Peter Parley's Universal History*—not merely *a* Volume Two, but *the* Volume Two, bearing on its flyleaf the
signature of Jason Peebles.

Despite these incidents, any discussion of the odd volume
must be based on the hypothesis (in which there is little
element of the hypothetical) that an odd volume never finds
its true mate—the companion with which it set out on the
ruinous journey that was to spell disaster to one and therefore to both. Is it, then, reasonable, ethical, sentimentally
sound to match a Volume One to a Volume Two to which it
has obviously never before been joined in wedlock? The fact
of mismating is almost always glaringly patent even to the
nontechnical eye; a matched set of a Cooper novel, of *Uncle
Tom's Cabin*, fairly screams its unhallowed status. No two
sets of units undergo an identical sequence of experiences,
are confronted by a parallel group of physical phenomena.
Perhaps no two of us even hold a book exactly alike, and the
structure of the book, though the book may conceivably
remain a fine copy, will somehow not only accommodate
itself to the manner in which it is held, but will make mani-
fest the way in which it accommodates itself—certainly to
the extent that two copies of the same edition, or two volumes of a set, will disclose distinctions of custodianship to
the alert collector.

Now it was, of course, sheer chance that first brought a
given Volume One and a given Volume Two together in the
first place. Up to the original casual juxtaposition in bindery
or stockroom, neither was definitively destined for the other,
any more than a specified gathering of sheets is ever pre-
ordained to constitute a single volume. The latter condition,
indeed, has produced many familiar bibliographical puzzles
of a superior order.

Once the set has gone out into the world, however, it is
technically as indissoluble as a single volume. Thereafter

any rearrangement of its component parts becomes as egregious a bit of tampering as the substitution of a signature from another volume. The substitution or insertion of a signature or a page is in most cases frowned upon by the cognoscenti, and properly, yet the grafting of wanting leaves from a hopelessly imperfect copy has the sanction of long tradition, and is certainly as respectable a procedure as the patching of a Tudor bedstead. But the book has to be rare and costly to lend the procedure the dignity it has acquired, and the fact of substitution must, of course, be proclaimed and not concealed. And thereby what would be at worst a fraud and at best a total destruction of sentimental and commercial value in the instance of a *Scarlet Letter* or a *Raven* or a *Way of All Flesh* becomes an accepted bibliophilic convention where a Caxton or a Shakespeare folio or a *Pilgrim's Progress* is concerned. It all sounds suspiciously like class legislation, and it is.

The matching of odd volumes, however, hardly involves the same quality of subterfuge—and the definition of subterfuge is here intended to be sufficiently broad to include deliberate self-deceit. Conceding, as this discussion does, the impossibility of actually bringing the original pair or trio or quartette together again, the collector must accept the next best thing: to wit, a set matched as closely as may be.

It is a paradox of book collecting—a paradox of which the acceptance is made inevitable by circumstance—that the matching of Victorian novels in parts is eminently permissible. No one buying a *Pickwick* or a *Vanity Fair* supposes for a moment that he is acquiring the identical nineteen periodical issues that were bought month by month by John Smith of the Hammersmith Smiths at a shilling each a century ago. On the excessively rare occasions when a "pure" set—the technical designation—appears in the auction room much is made of the fact of purity.

Some years ago a New York bookseller, after much searching on behalf of a Melville collector, secured from one out-of-town correspondent a copy of Volume One of *Clarel* and, a few days later, by a lucky chance, a copy of Volume Two from another. *Clarel,* true to the trade fashions of the 70's, originally appeared in cloth of various hues—blue, terra-cotta, green, perhaps others. The idea seems to have been to add a little gaiety to the retailer's shelves, and thereby to ensnare the roving emptorial eye. The sequential volumes that reached the New York bookseller were bound, unfortunately, the one in blue and the other in terra-cotta cloth, and while the 70's had approved mosaic shelf displays, they did not carry the style so far as to have the scheme apply within the individual set. The blue–terra-cotta set, a sort of heaven-and-earth combination, was a vivid bit of miscegenation, but, in default of a better, the bookseller offered it to the collector with the recommendation that he take it—at, of course, a figure attuned to the chromatic variety of the bindings. The collector declined the offer. This was, as we say, some years ago, and the collector may since have found a set nearer to his heart's desire, but *Clarel* is a genuinely rare book, and he may still be waiting.

Even if only a single copy of a book survives, that copy may multiply into a spurious commonness if it changes hands publicly a sufficient number of times. The discussion a few pages back of Stephen Crane's *Maggie,* for instance, disclosed the fact that two copies had each made two auction appearances within a few years of each other.

Auction cataloguers legitimately make a great to-do in describing an item of which five copies are known whereof four are in permanent public or semipublic collections, but every auction-house executive shudders none the less at mention of an institutional collection. The endowed library is an insatiable maw into which is fed valuable literary property that (it has until recently been assumed) can never again be vended. An auctioneer's heaven would be a spot peopled solely by a multitude of wealthy raveners for an uncut and inscribed quarto *Hamlet* who acquired it successively, each dying suddenly the following week after drawing up a will specifying that his books be dispersed at public sale.

The demand for rare books, which has multiplied in recent years with the growth and development of new colleges and universities both here and abroad, has been a factor in some institutions' wise decision to offer to the public duplicate material. The Newberry Library of Chicago did this when they acquired the famed Louis Silver collection in 1965. Indiana University pioneered the field in 1962 when it offered some duplicate books for public sale at New York's Parke-Bernet Galleries with conspicuous success. The foreword to the catalogue read:

> *Indiana University hopes to accomplish two things by offering duplicate books from the Lilly Library at public auction. Since the books herein described came to the University as unrestricted gifts, the sale will afford our other friends and patrons from the book world an opportunity to acquire titles that are increasingly difficult to obtain. Secondly, funds realized from this sale will be used to increase the resources of the Lilly Library, thus making it more useful both to the University and to the community of scholars.*
>
> *The choice of copies to be offered for sale involved bibliographical decisions of some weight. In general, the degree of completeness, the factor of association, and comparative condition governed the final selection. A few examples: The copy of Chaucer's* Canterbury Tales *printed by Caxton and retained in the Lilly Library is the Heber-Bright-Ashburnham-Bennett-Pierpont Morgan copy, more complete than the Ashburnham-Utterson copy described in this catalogue. The Kern copy of* Rubáiyát *of Omar*

Khayyám is offered for sale; it is a better copy than the one now in Lilly, but the latter is one of the few known presentation copies. The copy of Johnson's Dictionary offered is in contemporary calf; the copy retained by the Lilly Library is in original boards, uncut.

It is hoped that the action of Indiana University in disposing of these duplicate books will serve to advance the art of book collecting. Many college and university libraries count great resources today because of the generosity of the book collector and the labor of the bookseller. This sale is a slight gesture of recompense to that noble fraternity.

The factors that make a rare book rare are, first and most important, a demand in excess of the supply; the fact that only a few copies were printed; suppression, for whatever reason (but partially successful suppression); absorption by libraries and institutions; fragility of construction; accidental or premeditated destruction, for whatever reason and by whatever means, and the general wastage to which even the most substantially manufactured books are inevitably subject with the passage of the years—the way of all books as of all flesh.

■

CHAPTER FOUR

THE
FACTOR
OF
CONDITION

■

"All books are sold as catalogued, and are assumed to be in good secondhand condition. If material defects are found not mentioned in the catalogue, the lot may be returned."

So reads one of the conditions of sale—and a most important condition—in the front of the book catalogues issued by a great New York auction house.

What is good secondhand condition? Something, obviously, short of perfection. A book in good secondhand condition may show signs of having been read, but it should not show signs of having been maltreated. The binding, which makes the book rather farther than clothes make the man, should not be rubbed, scratched, stained, faded, bent or dog-eared. If the book be a highly valuable one, any defect in the binding will lower the value substantially. One of the most vulnerable points in a binding, as in any vertebrate creature, is the backbone. The top of the backbone, or backstrip, or shelfback, just above the name of the book, is peculiarly susceptible to mistreatment. If books are packed tightly on a shelf and an unthinking person tries to remove one by pulling his finger against the top of the backstrip, the backstrip is certain to tear, and the book is hopelessly damaged at its most conspicuous point. (Therefore, allow the books on your shelves room to breathe.) The body of the book should fit snugly into the binding. Misuse tends to loosen the body from the outer garment, and such a condition is difficult to repair. Repairs of any kind, furthermore, do not enhance the value of a rare book, and are resorted to only as a preservative.

The inside of the volume should be clean and whole. Again no harm is done, nor is the value of a book collector's item impaired, if the text shows signs of having been read. A book is not in good secondhand condition if the pages are badly smudged, or, worse yet, made hideous by marginal notes. Tobacco ashes—especially ashes hot enough to scorch the paper or even to burn holes through it—and gingerbread crumbs that leave an unmistakable trail of grease do not enhance the value of a rare book.

The endpapers—the blank leaves at the beginning and end of a book—should not bear writing, and writing on the title page is, of course, a supreme offense, unless the inscription carries some association interest. Rudyard Kipling's custom of inscribing his books by crossing out his printed name on the title page and inserting his name in ink is quite another thing from the usual "Cousin Harry from Frank" inscription. But there is something to be said, we think, for Frank.

When you buy a new book, it is not likely to have any writing on the flyleaf. (We suppose the thing has happened, because far less probable repositories of scribblement are of authentic record—many a householder at Thanksgiving time has extracted soggy communications from the interior of a turkey, and names and addresses laboriously limned on eggshells have set wedding bells to ringing.) But one of your

first acts, after acquiring a new book, may well be the in-
diting of an inscription, either to establish your equity in it
or to proclaim yourself as its bestower on an identified or
unidentified beneficiary. With few exceptions (such as critical comment, market lists, recipes for muffins, and idle
pencilings of the telephone-booth and restaurant-tablecloth
school), flyleaf inscriptions denote either ownership or donor-
ship.

You present the book, and the recipient, unendowed with
those nuances of taste which governed your selection, stares
your gift horse in the mouth, and pastures it in an inacces-
sible recess on his shelves. The cavalcade of the years sweeps
by; your gift becomes a sought-for first edition (it was
Sister Carrie, or *The Virginian,* or *The Single Hound,* or *The
Catcher in the Rye*); your depraved acquaintance projects
an indefinite stay in Tahiti, and his bookshelves are emptied
into the marketplace, whether bookshop or auction room
makes no matter. Your offering of an earlier day—unread,
unfingered, firm, intact—is duly catalogued: "As fresh as
when issued. Beautiful copy save for inscription on flyleaf."

The conviction has grown upon us as season has followed
season that the convention of the deleterious inscription is
the most illogical crotchet in the canon of book collecting.
Is it anything more than a survival that persists in the face
of rationality, like the buttons on a man's jacket sleeves?
Precisely wherein consist its potentialities for harm?

The casual inscription often has a bibliographic value for
which the scientific investigator is grateful. If the just-cited
bestowal by Frank on Cousin Harry be dated Christmas,
1894, and is in a book which carries an 1895 date on the title,
the student may be sure that Frank acquired a reasonably
early copy; his handiwork may thus become a *point d'appui*
for further research.

The apparently irrelevant inscription, moreover, may prove

to be highly relevant. A presentation Emerson was picked up for a few cents not many years ago because the bookseller blandly passed over a flyleaf inscription signed "RWE." A superb copy of Hearn's *Some Chinese Ghosts,* described by the auction house that offered it as having "writing on flyleaf," went to an astute collector who recognized the signature as that of one of Hearn's most devoted friends and adherents in New Orleans—a man named in half a dozen biographies. A copy of one of the commoner condensed texts which Dickens used for his readings does not lose in sentimental value from having the inscription "Heard Mr. D. give this in Birmingham Thursday night. Was greatly disappointed," even if the signer was a nonentity.

But it is better that the endpapers be inscribed, however ineptly and by whatever nonentity, than torn out. False modesty, or Lord knows what other motive, often prompts a person disposing of a quantity of books to remove any marks of identification they contain, however innocuous those marks may be. One way to remove them is to erase them carefully; a less laborious method is to rip out the offending leaf—but oh, the difference to the book! An endpaper can be reinserted for a small amount by a good repairman, but it will not be the original endpaper, and, in cataloguing for sale a book so treated, an auction house or a rare-book dealer will note that fact in describing it. Any other defect will likewise be noted, "Binding slightly faded," "name neatly erased from title," "loose in binding," "one hinge broken," "library label removed from cover"—these and a dozen other descriptive entries tell their own story, and give the intending purchaser a good idea of the condition of the particular copy of a book in which he may be interested.

It goes without saying that the practice of pasting newspaper clippings, however interesting, however pertinent, on the inside covers or any other part of any book, authentic scrapbooks alone excepted, inevitably mars the collection value of a book. But every clipping thus assured of a dubious immortality—as certain an immortality as the injured book, provided the clipping is pasted down securely enough—is invariably read by him who runs. The perusal is often disappointing—why, one wonders, was such a fragment of ephemera selected for perpetuation? And sometimes otherwise.

Every bookseller is familiar with the slender sixteenmos of Harper's Black and White Series, published in the early 90's, the covers of most copies of which have turned to black and gray with the suns and dusts and handlings of two generations. The series included several titles by William Dean Howells, among them *The Parlor Car, The Sleeping Car,* and *The Albany Depot.* And in 1892 appeared *In the Vestibule Limited* by the late Brander Matthews, dedicated to Howells, not by name, but as the author of the three railroad extravaganzas listed above. *In the Vestibule Limited* concludes with a marriage ceremony performed in a Pullman stateroom by the Rev. Dr. Pennington, who does "hope that the papers will not get hold of it." "And thus, on the appointed day, Hallett Larcom and Anita Vernon were made man and wife, while the New York and Chicago Limited was rushing onward through the gathering night at a speed of nearly fifty miles an hour." Thus the final paragraph of the story and of the book.

A friend of ours was happy to acquire (for fifteen cents, we think) a copy of *In the Vestibule Limited* which contained this clipping (from an unnamed paper, but apparently of date nearly contemporary with the book) tipped in on the margin of page 93 (the last text page):

"Wedded on the Vestibule. Ticket Agent McIntosh Gets Married on a Rear Platform.—Quite a novel wedding took place on Thursday afternoon at Connorsville, Ind. Harry McIntosh, the ticket agent at that place for the Cincinnati,

Hamilton and Indianapolis Railroad, and Miss Mary Mullen of Rushville were married on the rear platform of the vestibule train which passes through Connorsville at 5:45 P. M. While the train was running from Rushville to the county line the ceremony was performed by the Rev. J. H. Macniel of Rushville. Lowell Spurrier officiated as best man, and Miss Pearl Hornaday as bridesmaid. The whole party went through to Cincinnati, and en route a banquet was given the bride and bridegroom by the railroad people. The wedding was a surprise to the relatives and friends of both parties."

Truth, it seems, gets its ideas from fiction and goes them one better. What was the subsequent career of the Harry McIntoshes?

That copy of a book is imperfect which should contain an errata slip but does not, or which should contain some other sort of explanatory slip but equally does not. Not all inserted slips have to do with the fallibility of authors, editors, or compositors. Often they are the equivalent of stop-press news, and take the place of the fudge boxes which are familiar to readers of metropolitan evening papers.

A pathetic and unusual example of an inserted slip concerned with other than errata is to be found in the first American edition of Charles Lever's last novel, *Lord Kilgobbin* (New York, 1872). Lever concluded *Kilgobbin* in January of that year at Trieste while gravely ill—he died there four months later. Mrs. Lever herself died while the novel was in press. In the New York edition the dedication is printed on a slip tipped in at the first text page which reads: "To the memory of one whose companionship made the happiness of a long life, and whose loss has left me helpless, I dedicate this book, written in breaking health and broken spirits. The task, that was once my joy and my pride, I have lived to find associated with my sorrow: it is not, then, without a cause I say, I hope this effort will be my last."

The question of books as sources of infection (physical) relates as much to the factor of condition as to any other consideration, and is therefore a proper subject for brief discussion here.

What is one to do who owns a First Folio Shakespeare, or even a Fourth, and is stricken with measles or whooping cough? Happily, most collectors will have already hurdled the age barrier behind which such perils are customarily sequestered. But there are other communicable diseases which are no respecters of adulthood, and rare books are sometimes exposed to them, and what shall the collector do then, poor thing?

Well, there is one counsel of despair which he ought not to adopt, and that is to put the exposed books in an autoclave. The word has a hybrid theological-inquisitorial air about it, as if it were compounded of auto-da-fé and conclave, and this derivation, while etymologically defective, is at least sentimentally sound. For an autoclave is a kind of high-hat double boiler in which streptococci *et id genus omne* have the living daylights stewed out of them.

But what an autoclave can do to a book! Listen to Dr. H. E. Smiley of the staff of the Charles V. Chapin Hospital at Providence, whose paper "Books—Shall They Be Sterilized?" was reprinted from the *Rhode Island Medical Journal* in a pamphlet certain to produce bibliophilic shudders:

> *It is impractical to sterilize books in the autoclave. To demonstrate this fact a new book was wrapped in several thicknesses of newspaper and sterilized in the autoclave at 15 pounds' pressure for 15 minutes. On removal, the book was found to have its covers warped and its binding loosened; its whole appearance was considerably altered.*

And it was probably screaming "Uncle!" all over the laboratory. Can the reader endure more of this sadistic chronicle? The worst is over:

> *Another experiment was tried. Sterile strips of filter paper*
> *were saturated with a live broth culture of (a) strepto-*
> *coccus hemolyticus, isolated from a case of scarlet fever*
> *and (b) staphylococcus albus, isolated from a boil.*
> *These strips were then placed (1) on the outside of a book*
> *and (2) between the leaves. The books were then sub-*
> *jected to the various treatments listed below, and at spaced*
> *intervals a small piece of each strip was cut off and*
> *cultured in broth.*

The detailed results of the treatments to which Dr. Smiley refers are presented in a table which need not be reproduced here. Suffice it to say that the strip test was applied to books kept at various temperatures (one was even stowed in an icebox) for from one to forty-one days, at the end of which time only one unregenerate cluster of staphylococci refused to be dispossessed. Dr. Smiley's general conclusions are:

> *1. Hemolytic streptococci, when present on the surface of*
> *a book, are no longer viable after three weeks' exposure to*
> *room temperature, and at higher temperatures are no*
> *longer viable after shorter periods of time. Staphylococci*
> *are apparently a little more hardy, for they live after*
> *exposure to room temperature for a longer time than do the*
> *streptococci.*

> *2. Hemolytic streptococci and also staphylococci, upon*
> *the leaves of a book, are no longer viable after four days,*
> *provided the temperature is 65° C.*

> *3. A safe general rule appears to be that books, not*
> *grossly contaminated, if left untouched in a warm room for*
> *a few months, are not capable of transmitting infection.*

4. Spore-bearing contaminants [anthrax, for example] are not included in this experiment.

These conclusions check with the practice of the Department of Health of New York City as cited in *The Care and Repair of Books,* by Harry Miller Lydenberg and John Archer of the New York Public Library.

It was our subsequent privilege to stand before the identical autoclave in which Dr. Smiley subjected his specimens to ordeal by steam. The autoclave is a copper drum about the size of a sugar barrel that roosts on iron pipe legs at a height convenient for the operator to load and unload it. At first glance, and at last as well, it bears a clumsy resemblance to Samuel Pickwick. When the operator has loaded it—it can easily house a complete set of Charles Paul de Kock—he shuts the door, bears down on a gadget that makes it impossible for the door to open unless it bursts open (which has been known to occur), and turns valves which admit steam under such pressure that hell—a scalding, unillumined, Miltonic hell—immediately becomes payable inside.

It was also our privilege, under Dr. Smiley's supervision, to inspect a book which had undergone acute sterilization (nontextual) in the autoclave. It would perhaps be unfair to identify it here, but we can say that it was a contemporary novel of the usual physical dimensions and chemical constituents. It looked pretty sick—not even the most sanguine of cataloguers would have cared to designate it a fair copy. But it was still a book. The covers, though warped, were firmly affixed; the leaves were somewhat damp-curled, but there was little staining. The most interesting phenomenon was that while the steam had caused a rubber-stamp impression on the flyleaf to fuzz and run, the ink of the text was unharmed—the book was as readily readable as if the sheets had just left the press.

Dr. Smiley's findings, as given in his pamphlet, should

allay all fear of books as conveyors of disease if the simple precautions which he specifies are taken. But there is much research yet to be done (and an attractive study it ought to make) in the history of the fear of books as vehicles of pestilence since suspicion was first directed toward them— and when may that have been? Holbrook Jackson's *The Fear of Books* has nothing to offer on the topic—Mr. Jackson is concerned with queasinesses inspired by the inwards rather than by the outwards of books, with inherent rather than with acquired potentialities for harm. Nor does he appear to discuss the business in his compendious *Anatomy of Bibliomania*—a statement ventured with reservations, for the *Anatomy* is eminently a dippable book, and we may not have dipped at the right place.

There must somewhere be an allusion—perhaps a multitude of allusions—to the fear of books during the Great Plague of London, but Samuel Pepys seems nowhere to refer to this specific application of the emotion (which statement also is set down with reservations). Under September 20, 1665, Pepys notes that the roster of the stricken has reached 7,165, an increase of six hundred in a week—"what a sad time it is to see no boats upon the river; and grass grows all up and down White Hall court, and nobody but poor wretches in the streets!" Yet on October 5 he accepts from John Evelyn a copy of Evelyn's translation of Gabriel Naudés's *Instructions Concerning the Erecting of a Library*. And on December 18, within a week of his noting another increase in the number of sufferers, he "walked as low as Ducke Lane, and enquired for some Spanish books." Yet not until the following February 4 did this most timorous man of his day venture to take his wife to church (though he had often gone alone in the interval)—"it was a frost, and had snowed last night, which covered the graves in the churchyard, so as I was the less afraid of going through."

Nor is the bookworm cause for special terror to the collector. At all events there is no little gray home in the West for this once moderately formidable parasite. During a single year, according to the Huntington Library's seventh annual report, some 45,000 units in the superb repository at San Marino—books, maps, newspapers, and manuscripts—were put through the fumigation chamber and emerged sterile.

The report discloses that "the pest was not confining its ravages to old volumes but was attacking comparatively modern books as well." The bookworm, it appears, long infamous as no respecter of age, is equally no respecter of youth. Or of any other attribute. Some time ago a modest but competent New York expert was called upon (not, it should be added, by the Huntington Library) to inspect a collection of books which were alleged to have suffered severely at the hands (or is it the jaws?) of *anobium pertinax* or one of his burrowing brethren. The lady who owned the books bestowed on the expert a look that was designed to burrow through him.

"You are not an authority in these matters," she asserted. "You are not accustomed to handling treasures of such value—you are a mere junk dealer."

"Madam," retorted the expert equably, "that could be, but I have never heard it said that a bookworm made any distinction between a ten-thousand-dollar book and a ten-cent book."

Certainly no such distinction is made at the Huntington Library. Indeed, without knowing too much about it, we assume that the afflicted modern book is hustled into the operating room ahead of the rest, since it must offer a more fertile feeding- and hence breeding-ground than its sturdy forebears.

Not even the Huntington experts, however, have yet been able to devise a lethal chamber for the occupancy of human bibliophagi. A single picker-up—or, worse, a dropper-down—of a considerable trifle can inflict vast damage, but the accumulated caresses of a thousand reverers of a unique Elizabethan quarto, no matter how tender their ministrations, can do as much hurt. The solution of the difficulty is the photostatic copy, of which the Huntington has thousands —that is, *books,* exclusive of broadsides, letters, and comparable pieces the photomechanical reproduction of which involves little more difficulty than the taking of a snapshot.

Now the photostating of a rare book may appear at first glance to strike a root blow at collecting, if one takes the position, as many of us do, that the true collecting spirit has its basis in sentiment. But a great research library properly has no room for sentiment. Behind its array of glass cases and special exhibits, it is a beehive of scholarly endeavor, and scholars, at all events while they are endeavoring, have to be as unemotional as dentists or three-cushion billiard players. A photostatic facsimile serves the scholar's purpose as well as the original—even better, because if his fountain pen inadvertently lives up to its name he can blot the maculations and go right on investigating without fear of thrombosis. If the investigator's specialty is paper or type, or if he is trying to solve such a bibliographic puzzle as the impression of the "Finis" in the first edition of Gray's *Elegy,* he has a logical reason to view the original, and in such a library as the Huntington his logic will be respected and reciprocated.

The photostatic reproduction of a rarity is not in actual fact the body-thrust at sentiment which it seems. On the contrary, the practice heightens and halos the emotional quality inherent in the original. It takes the original out of the laboratory and enshrines it in the cathedral. Obviously the quantity of rarities which are likely candidates for reproduction has an appreciable limit—a limit pretty much determinable by the figure the units would bring if by some miracle they could regravitate to the auction room. Most of them are books which the average bibliophile gladly relinquishes to the skilled custodianship of the institutional collection. Recent years have seen an enormous increase in the number of such reproductions, and some, especially of notable medieval manuscripts, brilliantly done in full color, are published at prices often ranging well into hundreds of dollars. In the case of the Gutenberg Bible there has even been a facsimile *of* a facsimile of the entire work.

A perfect copy of a book is likely to be described as a "mint copy" (a term at which some cataloguers cringe) or "in pristine state." Perfection of perfection occurs when a book is uncut and unopened. The word "uncut" is probably the most misunderstood and misinterpreted term in the language. To anyone not familiar with its technical application, it is assumed to mean that the leaves have not been separated. A book in which the leaves have not been separated is described as unopened—a copy, in other words, which has not been prepared for reading. Uncut means simply that the edges of the sheets have not been trimmed.

The term "uncut" has lost much of its significance in recent years. It has little bearing in the case of modern authors —and contemporary and nearly contemporary writers are now in greater collecting demand than at any time in the history of collecting. Uncut as a descriptive term is now useful chiefly in describing old books which have been rebound in elaborate bindings. In rebinding a book the binder is usually forced to shave or trim the edges of the sheets, reducing their size sometimes to an appreciable extent, and impairing the appearance, if the trim is very deep, by making the margins narrower. Occasionally the binder commits the sin of sins, and cuts into the very text. An uncut, or only slightly cut, copy of a book is often described as a "tall copy," meaning that it has suffered less at the binder's hands than the general run of copies in the same edition. If the book be an especially valuable one, such a copy will command a substantial premium over the ordinary copy.

Most current books are published with all edges cut or with the side and lower edges uncut—a book with all three exposed edges uncut is an awkward thing to read, and the rough top edges make the finest dust trap in the world. A contemporary book in its original binding which sells at a collection premium is worth its price regardless of the state of the edges, provided those edges are in the state of original issue.

We say that the term "uncut" has lost much of its significance in recent years for the reason that nowadays collectors are more eager for books in their original bindings than in the elaborate finery of full crushed levant. By this we mean no disparagement of fine bindings. Some books are valuable for their bindings alone, and deservedly so. And the original bindings of many books are in such poor condition that only rebinding can properly preserve them—and the new dress should be as fine and as appropriate as the owner can afford to make it. But when a book worth $100, reattired in crushed crimson levant morocco, with gilt back, gilt fillet borders, inside dentelles and gilt edges—binders, it will be noted, speak a language all their own—sells for $1,000, it is usually the binding that makes the price, not the book. One may love beautiful bindings, and welcome to his shelves beautiful examples of the work of superb craftsmen of an earlier day or of his own—the brothers Eve, Le Gascon, Mearne, Payne, Cobden-Sanderson, Lortic, Pagnant—and still be eager above all else for first editions in the original bindings, be his objective Milton's *Paradise Lost* or Hemingway's *For Whom the Bell Tolls*.

The printed book as a fabricated entity is the same today as it was half a millennium ago. The Gutenberg Bible of 1455 or thereabouts differs in no structural essential from the Bruce Rogers Bible of 1935. Through all this span there is to be recorded only one radical departure in the involved economy of book production. For less than 150 years has the book left the hands of the publisher in the state in which it was designed to reach the owner.

The explanation is cloth. The discovery of the adaptability of cloth to the casing of books was of more epochal significance in publishing than the invention of the linotype. "It threw back on the publisher," declares John Carter in *Publisher's Cloth: An Outline History of Publisher's Binding in England, 1820-1900* (1935), "a function of book production which had hitherto lain in the province of the retailer." For previously, "from the earliest days of printing down to the beginning of the nineteenth century, the normal condition of any book during its wholesale period of existence was one of unblushing nakedness."

The bibliographical implications of the great transition are obvious. Virtually every Shakespeare First Folio possesses a distinct individuality to a degree that every copy of a Victorian three-decker does not. The contemporary purchaser of a First Folio had his copy tailored to his own inclinations. Thus, while a copy of a fifteenth-through-eighteenth-century book in its *original* binding is hardly an uncommon phenomenon, a copy of such a book *as issued* is, in the instance of most titles, unknown and doubtless forever unknowable.

Mr. Carter's "brief interim report of work in progress"— it stems from his *Binding Variants in English Publishing* (a unit in the essential Bibliographia Series)—offers in brief compass an adequate and understandable survey of a field with which every collector and student of the book owes it to himself to be familiar. Mr. Carter himself compresses his ten-thousand-word discussion into a thumbnail history of cloth (that is, edition) binding:

(1) *Origins and the primitive style.*   182?–1831

(2) *The struggle for recognition.*   1832–1840

(3) *The establishment of supremacy.*   1841–1855

(4) *The expansion of the fabric range.*   1856–1870

(5) *Variations on the technically perfect
     instrument.*   1871–1900

This table would doubtless parallel in the main the history of publisher's cloth in America.

As an example of how much more valuable a book is in the original binding, note the difference in price of two copies of the same book as given some years ago in the catalogue of a rare-book dealer.

> DARWIN, CHARLES. *On the Origin of Species by Means of Natural Selection, or the Preservation of Favoured Races in the Struggle for Life.* London: John Murray, 1859. $225. 12mo, First edition, original green cloth. A superlative copy with the gilt lettering fresh and the endpapers uncracked.
>
> ——The Same. Contemporary full green morocco, gilt edges. $50.

The first copy, in the original binding, "superlative . . . with the gilt lettering fresh" . . . etc. is worth over four times as much as the second. The green cloth on its binding cost perhaps one twentieth of the full green morocco. But the importance of original state outweighs all this.

An unopened book is the scorn of the unbeliever in collecting. What, a book that no one has ever troubled to read, or to prepare to be read? A book which the buyer would on no account "open"—which he will always leave in the virgin state in which he found it? Well, for the peace of mind of all concerned, it can be said that unopened books of any considerable maturity are rarely met with—that a person who set out to make a collection of exclusively unopened books would not only gather a most heterogeneous assortment, but would have considerable difficulty in gathering it. A book may be "opened" and, if nothing else is the matter with it, still be in superfine condition. This is assuming, of course, that the opening has been neatly done. Among the wrongs inflicted upon books that should be included among capital crimes is the offense of opening them with the fingers, with resulting great gouges in the margins.

There is one greater sin—removing the title page. The title page is the heart, soul, brain, the without-which-nothing of any book. One might assume that only a person actuated by the deepest malice could be capable of such an offense as ripping out a title page, and the assumption would be reasonable in this enlightened age. But in an earlier day—two and three hundred years ago—title pages were collected in England just as scalps were being simultaneously collected in America, forms of bibliological and anatomical synecdoche that were no more disastrous to the human beings concerned in the latter instance than to the books which suffered in the former. That is generally why the description of an ancient book offered at auction will sometimes bear the hideous confession "lacks title"—and it must be a rarity indeed to be worth putting up at auction after such a supreme act of mayhem.

There is sometimes an interesting cause behind the effect of a mutilated book—even of a book that lacks a title page. George Moore's *Pagan Poems* (London, 1881) is said to have so displeased its author when he saw it in print that he sought to suppress the edition, and did so by removing with his own hands the title page of every volume he could get hold of. Since Moore himself was supposedly guilty of this act of cruelty to one of his early children, may not the thesis be advanced that every copy of *Pagan Poems* is an association copy? And Percy Bysshe Shelley removed from every copy of his *Queen Mab* (London, 1813) that he could lay his hands on the dedication to his wife Harriet.

Consider, too, *Certaine Learned and Elegant Workes of the Right Honorable Fulke Lord Brooke, Written in his Youth, and familiar Exercise with Sir Philip Sidney,* printed in London in 1633. Pages 1–22 are missing in all known copies. "They contained," says a catalogue description, "a tract which has been carefully suppressed, usually believed to have been a treatise on religion unwelcome to the ecclesiastical authorities." A copy of the book with pages 1–22 in place would be a discovery, but suppression in the seventeenth century meant suppression, and Fulke Greville would doubtless have been grateful to see his book allowed to appear at all, even with one of the "elegant workes" removed. There is a sort of association value to the book, mutilated as it is, for it is a vivid reminder of a day in which Censorship was spelled with a capital C.

The craze for old colored maps has caused the spoliation of scores of books, just as many fine prints have won their way to the dignity of framing only at the expense of a divorce from the books in which they originally appeared. This type of divorce involves no alimony, but it does raise hob with the value of the book. But maps and prints are not always the prey of the picture hunter. Sometimes, especially if they are folded, their link with the book is somewhat tenuous, and, unless they are accorded the best of care, their disappearance is only a question of time. The practice of extra-illustrating books has been responsible for the destruction or serious mutilation of many books. It takes many moles to make a moleskin coat, but it takes many more books to make an elaborate extra-illustrated book.

It is almost impossible to find some first editions in pristine condition. This is true of children's books, for obvious reasons. *Alice in Wonderland* (1865), *Tom Sawyer* (1876), and *The Wonderful Wizard of Oz* (1900) appealed originally to an audience that was not especially schooled in the care of books, which is why they are hard to find today in good condition, or in any condition at all.

The question of condition must involve some consideration of the dust jacket. To many booksellers the dust jacket is a poisonous subject, and even the collector who goes almost to the point of putting the jacket ahead of the book ought to be able to sympathize with the bookseller's position. We have said earlier in this chapter that the shelfback is the most vulnerable part of a book, but the dust jacket is even more vulnerable. But is the dust jacket a part of a book? Or is it a distinct entity? Most booksellers would answer the second query with an unequivocal yes.

The business could be debated endlessly, and probably will be, but not here. Our own conclusion is, after discussing it with numerous collectors, that the majority are opposed to paying a premium for a book merely because the jacket is present, but that few of them—only one of our acquaintance, to be exact—throw the jacket away if it is present.

The jacket itself, however, offers an interesting field for the collector who wants to specialize in it for its own sake. The literature of the jacket is singularly scant, and the collector who investigates it should soon find himself in the position of being an authority on the subject. He will find, we think, that the jacket has passed through six evolutionary stages, as follows (but the dating of these will have to await his researches):

1. *Plain unlettered protective wrapper.*

2. *Protective wrapper with name of book and author on face or backstrip or both, in plain type—a simple label.*

> *3. Protective wrapper with name of book and author displayed with some attempt at effectiveness—a stage above the mere label—and perhaps with an illustration from the book.*

> *4. Same as No. 3, with addition on back of wrapper (hitherto blank) of advertising text, but not about the book encased in the wrapper.*

> *5. Wrapper with an approximation of the blurb copy of today, plus an eye-catching layout.*

> *6. Same as No. 5, with addition of listings and descriptions of other books on back cover.*

Somewhere in this list a place may have to be made for the first wrappers to carry copy on the flaps. At present the most significant omission in the whole discussion is No. 5.

We do not know with certainty when the first dust wrapper appeared. The Lilly Library has a unique copy of the collected works of a minor English poet, Richard S. Gedney (London, 1857) which is certainly among the earliest on record. This reproduces the title page, and is otherwise blank. The book whose dust jacket carried the first blurb about the book itself obviously marked a milestone in the history of publishing.

The commercial aspect of the reason for the growth of wrappers is simple. In the latter half of the nineteenth century many books, especially juveniles, had highly decorated, attractive, and expensive bindings. It was soon discovered that it was cheaper to do an attractive dust wrapper than a similar binding, and the decline of the binding set in. The ultimate has been reached in paperbacks, where binding and illustrated dust wrapper with blurb are one unit.

Condition is the most important physical factor in any

THE

POETICAL WORKS

OF THE LATE

RICHARD S. GEDNEY,

OF AMERICA, LATTERLY RESIDENT IN ENGLAND.

Second Edition,

WITH NUMEROUS ADDITIONAL POEMS, AND A MEMOIR OF THE AUTHOR.

EDITED BY

JAMES OGDEN, M.D., M.A., PH.D., &c.

NEW YORK:
APPLETON AND CO., BROADWAY.
LONDON: WHITTAKER AND CO., AVE MARIA LANE.
MANCHESTER: GALT AND CO., DUCIE PLACE.
1857.

One of the earliest
known surviving dust wrappers.

collectible book. Wormholes may assist the value of old furniture, but they detract from the value of an old book. The closer a book approximates newness, the more desirable it becomes. A Gutenberg Bible that had been packed away in a dry (but not too dry) cedar closet on the day of publication, with the closet remaining sealed until its contents was prepared for the exhibition that precedes public sale, would be worth more than any other Gutenberg Bible in existence.

PART II

■

THE CHASE

■

■

CHAPTER FIVE

THE
MECHANICS
OF
COLLECTING

■

It is the collector's business to know what he wants. Few rare-book dealers would have the temerity to attempt to influence his tastes. Generally it would be poor business to do so. The rare-book dealer is the one man in the world who cannot have a favorite author—or, if he has one, must keep him under cover.

As a day-to-day student of the situation, however, the dealer can supply the collector with information which the collector himself, unless he is in the fortunate position of being able to devote his full time to his hobby (which then ceases to be a hobby), might not hear about—or might not hear about in time to take advantage of.

Once a reader has decided to become a collector, how does he go about it? It would be interesting, by the way, to compile the reasons why a hundred different collectors were won to their hobby. Probably no book collector ever became so by pure induction—by inferring from any haphazard edition of a book that obviously that book existed in the beginning in a first edition, and that it would be a fine idea to have a copy of that first edition.

What kind of people collect books is an interesting subject. It is rather surprising that publishers, editors, and scholars are rarely collectors, as priority of editions has some technical significance to them. Printers, on the other hand, have been notable collectors, witness Robert Hoe. However, publishers are forward-looking people, and have to be if they are going to stay in business and remain solvent. Publishing is, they say, "the worst business in the world," and its problems are never solved. A half-century ago they were certain that the bicycle craze was corrupting youth to the point where everyone would grow up illiterate, if healthy, and publishing was doomed. A generation later it was automobiles and movies, nontalking. (On these at least you had to read captions.) Still later it was radio, then talking pictures, and now television, all driving the nation into illiteracy, and publishers into bankruptcy. This is one reason why publishers are not antiquarians. They are not interested in their past, from which they could learn a lot, mainly because they are so frightened of their future.

Editors are not antiquarians either—at least I never knew one who was; they are too concerned with next year's books to worry about past years' achievements. They have, as Scribner's Editor Burlingame has put it, "to tease, cajole, humor, placate and scold angry and brooding men and women who have found a superfluous semicolon or refused to believe a royalty report, or searched the *Times* in vain for an advertisement or been unable to buy a copy of their precious book at a bookstore." It's a full-time job being an editor, and they are interested in next year's book, not last year's.

Again, scholars generally are not collectors, though some are antiquarians. They are thorough examiners of the treasures others have accumulated but they seldom do the accumulating themselves, and they are capable of driving librarians to the verge of distraction by their insatiable demands for research material. But this is understandable because their job is interpretation, not accumulation.

Nor does the novelist usually collect books. He is too busy trying to write them, and after supporting a family and paying taxes he hasn't much left to collect books with. It was not so many years ago that Hawthorne (Julian) said:

> I will engage to entertain at dinner, at a round table five feet in diameter, all the American novelists who make more than a thousand dollars a year out of the royalty of any one of their novels, and to give them all they want to eat and drink, and three of the best cigars apiece afterwards, and a hack to take them home in; and I will agree to forfeit a thousand dollars . . . if $25 does not liquidate the bill and leave enough over to buy a cloth copy of each of the works in question, with the author's autograph on the fly-leaf.

And times haven't changed much, despite occasional bonanzas from television, moving pictures, and book clubs. What with inflation, though, "three of the best cigars apiece" might dent Hawthorne's $25 severely. There have been notable exceptions to noncollecting authors—Walter de la Mare, Hugh Walpole, John Drinkwater, Amy Lowell, George Barr McCutcheon, Carolyn Wells, Christopher Morley, Vincent Starrett. Possibly, to paraphrase Charles Lamb, most authors, like publishers and editors, are more interested in tenth than in first editions. Generally speaking, collectors do not follow their professional interests in their hobbies, e.g., musicians do not collect music, nor lawyers legal works.

The exception (and there always is one) is doctors. They are, as a class, more devoted bibliophiles than are the members of any other profession, and they tend to collect works on medicine. Indeed Conrad Gesner's *Bibliotheca universalis* (1545–1555) is known as the father of bibliography, and three and a half centuries later Sir William Osler used it as one of the models for his own description of his famed medical collection, *Bibliotheca Osleriana*.

How does a collector collect? The operation may perhaps best be described by giving the story of a hypothetical collector.

Let us assume that one John Smith is attracted to the work of Stephen Crane by reading *The Red Badge of Courage*. It may be that Mr. Smith, who, though a young man of considerable formal education, makes no elaborate pretensions to wide or deep knowledge, had never before heard of Crane —some thousands of normally intelligent citizens had not before the publication of Thomas Beer's biography. Smith chanced on *The Red Badge of Courage*, perhaps, in an American Library Association copy while he was a soldier in France—and the fact that many copies found their way into the service in both World Wars, as Vincent Starrett points out, is undoubtedly one of the reasons why the first edition of *The Red Badge of Courage* (1895) is such a scarce book today.

The fighting ended, and Smith forgot all about books in the excitement of looking forward to the trip home. But that trip was still several months off; time dragged never so heavily, and Smith got to wishing he had something else by that man Crane. Nothing came to hand, so Smith spent the interval in rereading *Pickwick* and *The Last of the Mohicans*, and in further thumbing several already much-bethumbed copies of six-months-old magazines. For the actual journey home—which, after the passage of several seeming centuries, finally eventuated—he bought a copy of *Les Misérables*.

Home again in a New England town of ten thousand people, Smith found he had less time for reading than he had had while the war was actually in progress. He welcomed the renewed privileges of the home-town library, however, and one day happened to remember to consult the card catalogue for other Crane books. The library had *The Red Badge of Courage* and *Active Service*, which sounded attractive. *Active Service* proved not to have quite the appeal of *The Red Badge of Courage*, but Smith liked it. And it did serve to reawaken his interest in Crane, and to stimulate his zeal to read more Crane books.

One day Smith went on a business trip to a neighboring city of a quarter of a million people. He finished his errand, and had an hour or more until train time when he happened to pass an antiquarian bookstore. Good place to kill that hour. He scanned the shelves idly, having no particular objectives in view. (This was a bookstore like the honored Leary's in Philadelphia, where a customer is not buttonholed on his entrance and asked if he wants "anything special.") Smith happened to think of Crane. Better ask the proprietor.

"Crane? No, not a thing, I'm afraid. Yes, wait a minute."

Business of toddling off to some secret recess and returning therefrom holding a book that bears a striking external resemblance to *The Red Badge of Courage*.

Smith holds in his hands a copy of *The Little Regiment*. Attractive title. Same binding as *The Red Badge of Courage*, hence, by natural if unsound inference, the same kind of book.

"Guess I'll take this. How much?"

Smith reaches into a trousers pocket sheltering perhaps a dollar in loose change.

"Ten dollars."

"Ten—*dollars?*"

"Yes. You see, it's a first edition."

Smith had not seen that it was a first edition. Smith would have been unable to tell that it was a first edition. Now that it was pointed out to him as a first edition, that fact meant nothing to him. To Smith it was just a second-hand book.

"Well, I didn't want to pay anything like that. Haven't you a cheaper one? Why, this book couldn't have cost more than two dollars when it was new."

"I doubt if it cost as much as two dollars when it was new," replies the bookseller, smiling, convinced that this apparently unsophisticated young man actually is unsophisticated.

"Then why is it worth so much now?"

"Because it's a first edition."

The argument has got back to the starting point with Smith little the wiser, so the dealer goes into first principles.

"A book, you see, may be printed many times, like the Bible or Shakespeare's plays or *Moby-Dick*. But whether it is printed many times or not, to be a book it has to be printed a first time. A copy of the first printing of a book is a copy of the first edition. And there are a lot of people who like to collect first editions."

"I see," says the enlightened Smith. "So a first edition of a book is always worth a lot of money."

"Not always. You might even say less often than not. See those shelves of cheap fiction? Half of them are probably first editions, yet they sold new for a few dollars."

"Then how do you tell what first editions are worth anything?"

"A first edition is worth something if somebody wants it badly enough to pay the price, and the price, like the price of wheat or eggs, is determined by the quantity available, the number of consumers who want part of that quantity, and how badly they want it. Just now Crane first editions are pretty popular. And they're scarce. I'm not a rare-book dealer—I'm just a secondhand book dealer. If I were a rare-book dealer I'd have disposed of this book months ago. As a matter of fact I ought to offer it to some rare-book dealer in New York, because there's little collecting trade here. I just keep a few first editions on hand, though, to show myself that I know one when I see one."

"Are all Crane first editions worth ten dollars?"

"No. The price varies with the rarity of the book and the demand for it. Some of his books sell for much less than ten dollars, some for a lot more."

"Is *The Red Badge of Courage* valuable? I shouldn't think it would be—it must have been a very popular book."

"*The Red Badge of Courage* is worth around sixty or seventy dollars, judging by some rare-book dealers' catalogues I've seen recently. Some ask around fifty, and I've seen it quoted well over a hundred if it was a fine copy."

Smith gasps. Was the copy of *The Red Badge of Courage* which he read in France a first edition? That question will vex him for the rest of his collecting life, which is to say the rest of his natural life.

"How can I find out about Crane first editions—what ones there are and how much they sell for?"

"Well, there's a book published every year called *American Book-Prices Current* which gives the figures of books sold at auction during the past season. Of course, if a book wasn't sold at auction during the season, you won't find a price quoted there. Then you can write to rare-book dealers in New York or Chicago or a dozen other American cities— to London if you want to—and get their catalogues. They're almost certain to have some Crane books on hand. They'll be glad to let you know what Crane books there are, whether they have them or not, and to be on the watch for copies for you."

"Can I find out somewhere what books Crane wrote? I suppose an encyclopedia would tell me."

"Yes, and you can find out from the dealers' catalogues to some extent."

It must be assumed that the dealer had not heard of Vincent Starrett's and Ames Williams' excellent bibliography of Stephen Crane—this in passing, because this will come in for extended mention later.

"Well," says Mr. Smith, "I've never bought a first edition before"—which is probably inaccurate, though Mr. Smith does not mean it to be—"and I may never buy one again. But I'll take this one."

And the business is done, concluding with the dealer's taking Smith's address and promising to let him know if any more Cranes come to the dealer's notice.

On the train journey home Smith unwraps his prize and opens *The Little Regiment* with the gingerly deference due to a mere book that has cost such an unconscionable lot of money. The title page, he notes, refers to Crane as "Author of *The Red Badge of Courage*, and *Maggie*," and the book is dated 1896. *The Red Badge of Courage*, then, was published no later than 1896, so Smith catalogues in his mind the fact that if he ever happens on a *Red Badge* dated 1897 or later, he will know that it cannot be a first edition. A rudimentary instance of bibliographical reasoning, perhaps, but of such rudimentary and common-sense principles does the highly exact science of bibliography consist. And *Maggie*. So Crane wrote a book called *Maggie*—not a very martial title alongside *The Red Badge of Courage*, *The Little Regiment*, and *Active Service*—and *Maggie* also was first published not later than 1896.

That evening Smith visits his hometown library and begins his investigation. Consulting first the *Encyclopaedia Britannica*, he reads that Crane's "first story, *Maggie, a Girl of the Streets*, was published in 1891, but his greatest success was made with *The Red Badge of Courage* (1896)." No mention of *The Little Regiment* or any other books, yet the secondhand dealer implied that there were several. Also, as Smith will learn later, both of the assigned dates are wrong.

In the *Encyclopedia Americana*, Smith finds a somewhat more extended notice. *The Black Riders, and Other Lines* (1895) is called Crane's "earliest volume." In addition to this, several other titles are given: *The Red Badge of Courage* (once more erroneously dated 1896), *Maggie* (1896), *George's Mother* (1896), *The Little Regiment* (1897, for 1896), *The Third Violet* (1897), *The Open Boat* (1898), *The Eternal Patience* (1898), *Whilomville Stories* (1900), *Wounds in the Rain* (1900), and *Great Battles of the World* (1901). "In 1903," declares this account, "appeared *O'Ruddy*, written in collaboration with Robert Barr." Two errors in dates in this list, one of which Smith recognizes; one error in title; one invented book—*The Eternal Patience*, of which Vincent Starrett has said: "Frequent mention is made by earlier writers about Crane to a book, supposedly a novel, called *The Eternal Patience*, a title that has given collectors no little trouble. No one appears ever to have seen a printed copy, although Victor G. Plarr, in his *Men and Women of the Time* (London, 1899), gives it a date—1898—and lists it as a published work. It is said to have been rejected by several magazines, and to have been withdrawn by Crane on one occasion when it had been partly set in type. What became of it is not known. Mr. Plarr, I may add, has never seen it, and has no idea where he got his information."

But Mr. Smith, were he aware of them, would pardon the shortcomings of the *Americana*, for his Crane list, including the so far unmentioned *Active Service*, has now swelled to thirteen titles.

So to *Chambers's Encyclopædia,* where he learns that "from 1891 Crane became known as an eccentric poet and novelist of promise"—definite implication that Crane books existed in 1891. *The Red Badge of Courage* is once more assigned an 1896 date, and eight other books are mentioned without dates, including two new titles, *The Monster* and *Active Service* (here entitled *On Active Service*). One candid error in date, one circumstantial error in date, one erroneous title. But Smith has fourteen titles.

In *Nelson Perpetual Loose-Leaf Encyclopedia* Smith reads that Crane "published privately *Maggie, a Girl of the Streets* (1891)" and that "in 1896 appeared *The Red Badge of Courage.*" "Privately" sounds interesting. Five other titles and dates are given, including one new one, *War Is Kind* (1899), though *The O'Ruddy* is again called *O'Ruddy,* and dated 1900 instead of 1903. Three errors in date, one in title. Fifteen titles now in Smith's list.

In Appelton's *Annual Cyclopedia* for 1900 Smith sees for the first time a portrait of Crane, who died in that year. "He first attracted attention," reads the accompanying obituary, "by *The Black Riders, and Other Lines* . . . issued in 1895, and followed this the next year with *The Red Badge of Courage.*" *Whilomville Stories* is referred to without date and nine other works with date, including that phantasmagorial production *The Eternal Patience*—1898 or bust. *Maggie: A Girl of the Slums* is news to Smith, as it would have been to Crane, though it may be mentioned in passing that the English edition has the title *Maggie, a Child of the Streets.* *War Is Kind* is correctly described as "a book of verse," though its appearance is pre-dated a year. Two errors in date, one error in title, one invented book.

The *National Encyclopaedia of American Biography* says

that *The Black Riders* appeared in 1895 and *The Red Badge of Courage* "the following year." *The Little Regiment* is mistitled *A Little Regiment*, is described as "a war story" instead of as a collection of war stories, and is misdated 1897 —error could hardly go further in such small compass. Fourteen titles are cited, including *The Eternal Patience* and *Dan Emmons* (1898). Even Mr. Starrett, who devotes two pages to works of which "some are believed to have been written and destroyed, some half written and destroyed or lost, and some merely to have existed in Crane's head," has no record of this title, which is ample proof to us (as it will be later to Smith) that *Dan Emmons* never existed. *The O'Ruddy* is again listed without the definite article and misdated 1900. Three errors in date, two in titles, one inaccurate description, two invented titles. To Smith's ears, however, *Dan Emmons* has the ring of authenticity, so down it goes on his list as a sixteenth title.

Now it will be noted that while each of these seven standard works of reference contains at least two serious errors, all make one mistake in common. How does it happen that in every instance *The Red Badge of Courage*, one of the most famous books of its decade, and an accepted classic of American literature, is dated 1896? We don't know, and whatever the explanation may be it will not suffice—the murder has been done. The situation is more than academic. Mr. Smith will have scores of opportunities to buy a *Red Badge* of 1896 for fifty cents or a dollar, and only one opportunity to acquire the first issue of 1895 for as low as forty dollars.

A happy inspiration leads Mr. Smith to consult the *Cambridge History of American Literature*. At the end of Volume IV is the most satisfactory bibliography in brief—the only satisfactory one, in fact—which he has so far come upon. Fourteen titles are given, all of genuine books, and all titles and dates are accurate—including *The Red Badge of*

Courage. Maggie is dated 1896, followed by the bracketed statement "privately printed 1893." When Smith is finally introduced to the Starrett-Williams bibliography he will find many more separate titles listed, but there is a distinction between a definite and all-embracing descriptive bibliography and a brief checklist, which is all that the *Cambridge History* designs or can be expected to give. At all events, the list provides a satisfactory target for Smith's ambitions at this stage of his collecting activities, and, noting the patent inaccuracies and discrepancies in the seven works of reference, he wisely inclines to the *Cambridge History*. With the vote seven to one for 1896 for *The Red Badge of Courage,* however, he will require further testimony in support of the 1895 date.

Before leaving the library, Smith looks in the advertising sections of half a dozen literary periodicals and the Sunday literary supplements of such big-city newspapers as publish them, culling therefrom the names of a dozen rare-book dealers—eventually his list will include addresses in New York, Chicago, Philadelphia, Boston, Providence, Washington, Baltimore, San Francisco, Los Angeles, and other cities large and small.

On the way home Smith reflects on the obvious inability of the mind to assimilate all existing data in the catalogue of human activity. Here is this man Crane, of whom, up to his introduction to him through *The Red Badge of Courage,* Smith had never heard. He might have written something else—doubtless few authors stopped at a single book, which reminded Smith of an old high-school jape that Shakespeare had written only one book: *The Complete Works of William Shakespeare.* Probably Crane had done three or four other things. And now Smith had the titles of sixteen separate works.

A dozen postal cards are forthwith dispatched to a dozen rare-book dealers. The cards in the mails, Smith has murmurings of doubt. He remembers how his father once answered an advertisement about a twenty-volume history of the world because a beautiful wall map in seventeen colors would be sent on request. The request was duly sent, and in response the map and a high-pressure salesman who had driven the helpless Mr. Smith Senior into a corner, permitting him to emerge only after he had signed an agreement to pay five dollars a month for an infinite number of months for the complete history.

Smith's forebodings subside as the "agents" fail to appear and the catalogues do. One of them is a mere mimeographed list—which is, of course, nothing to be held against the books offered, but represents a somewhat ineffective mode of salesmanship. The rest are neatly printed and bound booklets which make, severally and collectively, the most fascinating reading in the world. Smith turns first of all, naturally, to the Crane items. He finds that:

Two of the twelve catalogues list no Crane items at all.

Ten list a total of thirty Crane books (counting duplicates), ranging from seven which list a single item each to one that lists seven.

The thirty books embrace sixteen separate titles, as follows:

Seven catalogues list *George's Mother,* quoting it at from $3.50 to $7.50—the average price is around $5.

Four list *The Third Violet,* at from $5 to $10.

Three list *The Little Regiment,* two at $10 and one, to Smith's acute distress, at $7.50.

Two list *The Red Badge of Courage,* one at $50 and one at $125—some difference of opinion there!

Two list *A Souvenir and a Medley* (East Aurora, New York, 1896) at $12.50 and $15—news to Smith.

Two list *Maggie* (1896) at \$17.50 and \$20.

There are ten titles which appear only once each in the whole batch of catalogues. These are:

The Black Riders (1895)	\$25.00
The Open Boat (1898)	12.50
War Is Kind (1899)	6.00
Active Service (1899)	4.50
The Monster (1900)	10.00
Wounds in the Rain (1900)	7.50
Whilomville Stories (1900)	10.00
The Monster (London, 1901)	10.00
Great Battles of the World (1901)	10.00
The O'Ruddy (1903)	4.00

Smith is pleased with the familiar ring of these titles, though he is somewhat puzzled at the disparity in cost between the items, noting that, roughly, the cost varies inversely with the date of publication. Inspecting the list further, he notes that this roughness is somewhat too pronounced to be of any use in computing values. There must be some other reason—probably the cheaper titles are more abundant. He is also confused by the wide variations in prices which different dealers assign to the same items—he will learn, later, that there is no hard-and-fast rule by which the price of a rare book can be fixed. But he does notice that because Dealer A asks less for a given item than does Dealer B, it does not follow that Dealer B's quotation on Item Number 2 will be lower than Dealer A's.

Smith gets paper and pencil and computes what it would cost to buy every book in the list at the lowest quoted figure —every book he wants, that is, which means all except *The Little Regiment*. One hundred and seventy-eight dollars! Whew! Almost twice what Smith's pay envelope holds every Saturday! This book game certainly can't be played on a piker limit. Smith tosses the catalogues aside in disgust, and goes to bed.

But the next evening he is back at them again. After all, he ventured ten dollars on *The Little Regiment* when he knew much less about first editions than he knows today. Why not venture another ten dollars, spread out to cover as many Crane books as it can? So he selects *George's Mother* at $3.50, *The O'Ruddy* at $4, and *Active Service* at $4.50—a total of $12. Then he decides he won't get *Active Service* just now, having read it—when, if ever, he gets a chance at an 1893 *Maggie*, do you think he is going to risk chafing one of its flimsy corners by reading it?—and so he substitutes for it the $5 copy of *The Third Violet*. Twelve dollars and a half. Two and a half more than he meant to spend. Never mind.

The three books are ordered—they happen to be on the lists of three separate dealers—and duly arrive. Smith enjoys three distinct thrills, each of which is even more titillating than the thrill of looking over a catalogue. He is now the owner of a Crane collection—a modest one, to be sure, but a Crane collection nonetheless. Money orders are dispatched for *War Is Kind* (even though it is a book of verse) and *Wounds in the Rain*—$13.50. Mr. Smith is rapidly approaching the damn-the-expense stage.

Rapidly, but not precipitately. He still feels a reluctance to pay ten dollars for a book, even though he did do so once in a rash moment of sudden enlightenment. He feels an even greater reluctance to pay more than ten dollars for a book.

But a great piece of good fortune is about to befall Smith. A check for one hundred and fifty unanticipated dollars, a state bonus for his war service, falls into his lap. Simultaneously he is compelled to make a business trip to New York. Stuffing a few essentials (not least of which are the twelve book catalogues) into his bag, and placing the check in his billfold, he entrains. On the journey he goes over the catalogued Crane items in detail. He plans to visit as many rare-book dealers as possible, ask questions, seek advice, inspect books—courses of conduct that may not put him to the slightest expense. He is prepared, however, to spend money, and he is divided between two possible methods of spending it. Given one hundred and fifty dollars, shall he try to obtain therefore the greatest possible bulk, that is, buy all the five- and ten-dollar Crane items he can, and perhaps a few other things by other writers (he is a devoted admirer of Stevenson and Kipling), or shall he courageously seek out the more costly items?

He is still undecided when he enters the establishment of Dealer A. It is a modest place, modestly stocked. Dealer A is evidently a good sort—youngish, well dressed, not bespectacled, three details in which he differs completely from the picture of the old-fogy type of dodderer with which Smith had for some reason associated all rare-book dealers.

"Have you any books by Stephen Crane?" inquires Smith.

"Crane? Yes, I think so. Let's see. Here's *The Little Regiment, The O'Ruddy, George's Mother*—interested in any of those?"

"I'm sorry, but I have all of those," and what a superior collector Smith feels in saying that!

"Mm. Well. Sorry. Anyone else you're interested in?"

"No, not right now. Are you likely to have any more Cranes soon?"

"Can't say. I had a *Red Badge of Courage* up to a few days ago."

"Do you mind telling me what you sold it for?"

"One hundred and fifteen dollars, but it was in beautiful condition."

"So condition makes a difference in the price of books, does it?" Smith is about to ask, but he reflects in time that such a question would brand him as a sub-freshman in this business. He salts the fact away, however, and while he buys no books from Dealer A, he has received a pointer from that gentleman which advances his collecting *savoir faire* by many strides. As witness:

In reply to the formula "Have you anything by Stephen Crane?" Dealer B smiles apologetically.

"I haven't a thing," he says, "except a fair copy of *The Red Badge of Courage.*"

"May I see it?" asks Smith, to whom, up to ten minutes ago, "fair copy" would have meant legible handwriting.

The book is placed in his hands—one book worth, "in beautiful condition," one hundred and fifteen dollars, or almost as much as Smith's father had paid for all twenty volumes of that history of the world. The cover is somewhat soiled, the red and black letters are badly faded, the book seems to be loose in the binding, there is writing on the flyleaf: "Joseph from Uncle Albert, Christmas, 1895." There is the familiar title page, with the little ornaments spotted all over it—dated 1895. An additional little thrill runs through Smith—why, this might have been the very copy he had in France! He didn't recall Uncle Albert, but Uncle Albert might have been there all the same and escaped Smith's notice. Certainly the cover of the copy he had read had been as soiled and faded, the backbone as badly crinkled from the book's being folded, back cover against front cover, for convenience in reading in his bunk.

"No, it's not in very good shape, is it?" remarks Smith casually, recalling that this is the establishment whose catalogue priced *The Red Badge* at forty dollars.

Dealer C has the most pretentious shop which Smith has yet visited. The room itself is not garishly furnished, however, the pretentiousness of the place consisting in the long rows of shelves, reaching from the floor almost to the ceiling, filled with many thousands of books.

"What have you got by Stephen Crane?"

"Crane? Several things. Here they are—want to look them over? Just call me if I can help you."

And the proprietor goes back to his desk and is at once re-immersed in the day's business.

Smith likes this treatment. Dealers A and B were a little too assiduous. After all, this rare-book stunt isn't like buying clothes—you know what you want, and all the paternalism in the world won't influence you one way or the other.

Before him is the most imposing array of Crane books which Smith has yet set eyes on. A *Maggie* of 1896, dressed exactly like *The Red Badge of Courage*, *The Little Regiment*, and *The Third Violet* (the two last named are also present); *A Souvenir and a Medley*, protected by a Manila envelope (seems to be just a pamphlet); *The Open Boat*, and, strange to relate, another *Open Boat* that looks altogether different; *War Is Kind*; *Active Service*; *George's Mother*; *Whilomville Stories*; *Great Battles of the World*; *The O'Ruddy*. Twelve books, each with the price neatly and lightly penciled on the inside of the front cover.

But why the two *Open Boats?* Smith looks at the title pages. One is called *The Open Boat and Other Tales of Adventure*, the other *The Open Boat and Other Stories*. Both are dated 1898—hold on, one was published in New York and the other in London. Wonder what difference that makes? If a collector has to have the New York and the London editions of every book this game is going to cost just about twice as much as Smith thought.

"Oh, the London edition? That contains a lot of material that wasn't in the New York edition, I think. Let's see."

Mr. C consults a thin book from a shelf behind his desk.

"Here it is: 'This is an important first edition, containing as it does nine stories that did not appear in the N. Y. edition, which are here printed for the first time between covers.' This London edition, you see, is a first edition in its own right, not just the same text as the New York edition of the same year."

"I see," says Smith. "But what's that book you looked it up in?"

"That? Oh, that's the Starrett-Ames Williams bibliography of Crane. Haven't you a copy of that?"

The word *bibliography* stumps Smith. He has heard it before—that's what that list in the *Cambridge History* was called. Something to do with books, of course—lists of books—

"No, I haven't. Is it for sale?"

(This bibliography thing may be some sort of secret list, like those special timetables that railroad employees use, or the schedules of wholesale prices that any store has.)

"Yes, want one?"

A copy of the book is put in Smith's hands.

"Take it over to that Crane section and see if it works."

Smith turns the pages; his eye lights on *The Little Regiment*. That must be the title page at the top—but what are those little slanting lines? None of that in *The Little Regiment* itself. Ah! They show where the lines end on the actual title page: "THE LITTLE REGIMENT / And Other Episodes Of The American / Civil War / By / Stephen Crane / Author of The Red Badge of Courage, and Maggie / (publisher's device) / New York / D. Appleton and Company / 1896." That's exactly it, and all "in type similar to Old English."

But what's this? "Crown octavo; pp. vi + 196 + six pages of advertisements." Well, here are 196 pages of text, and here are six pages of advertisements—oh, that "vi" refers to the unnumbered pages in the front—title page and all that. Smith goes through the entire collation (as he later learns that such a Bertillonization of a book is called), and finds that the copy of *The Little Regiment* which he holds checks perfectly with the description in the bibliography.

"What does 'crown octavo' mean?" he asks Mr. C.

"Not much," smiles Mr. C. "It's a rough indication of the size of the book, based on the number of times the large sheets on which it is printed are folded. Such terms—folio, quarto, octavo, and the rest—nowadays have little significance, though the tradition persists, and you'll generally find them in bibliographies and in catalogues. But it's enough to know that a folio ought to be a pretty big book and a thirty-twomo a pretty small book. The octavos and twelvemos are the commonest sizes."

"You haven't a *Red Badge of Courage,* have you?" asks Smith.

"No, I haven't. That's a book that goes out of here about as soon as it comes in. In fact, I could use three or four copies right now."

"That's the most difficult Crane book to get hold of, isn't it?"

"No. Just turn to Number One in that bibliography."

And Smith reads:

" 'MAGGIE / A / Girl Of The Streets / (A Story of New York) / By / Johnston Smith / Copyrighted. . . . Issued in yellow wrappers. . . . This is Stephen Crane's first book, and is the keystone to any Crane collection. It is excessively scarce, and would seem never to have been placed on the market.' "

"That's it," says Mr. C. "You see he didn't use his own name—probably considered the story pretty daring in its realism, though it doesn't seem so to us. He probably wanted to know what people would say about it without knowing he had written it, so he had it printed at his own expense— no telling just how many."

"Is it worth very much today?"

"The last auction price was two hundred and seventy-five dollars. The next copy that comes up for sale is likely to bring considerably more. It's many times scarcer than *The*

Red Badge of Courage; it's a book you seldom see in any dealer's catalogue, because he's got so many customers waiting for it that he doesn't have to go to the trouble of cataloguing it—yet there's a chance (not a very great one, but still a chance) that you might pick it up in a trash pile somewhere for a nickel."

"You say a copy was sold at auction. Can you tell me something about auctions? I'm new to this book collecting business—started in a few months ago picking up Cranes. I live in Greendale, Massachusetts, and I don't get to New York very often. If you've got a few minutes to talk to me I'd appreciate it a lot."

Dealer C hands Smith a cigarette, lights one himself, and settles back in his chair.

"Auctions? Well, suppose a book collector dies, or decides to quit collecting, or to change from one group of authors to another, or just plain needs money, he or his heirs will dispose of his collection either to a rare-book dealer, like us, or at auction. From my point of view I think it's preferable to offer them to a dealer, but I can't deny I'm prejudiced.

"Selling books at auction is, of course, a gamble, especially for the owner of the books. They may bring marvelous prices, or they may bring next to nothing. Such an element as the weather has to be considered—auctions are held rain or shine, tornado or blizzard, and in very bad weather attendance, and therefore prices are likely to suffer. And suppose a rival auction house is conducting a more attractive sale the same day and hour. Not all dealers can cover both auctions, and prices are likely to be lower at the less attractive sale.

"One particularly unfortunate collector who had gathered over the years a very nice and representative collection of modern firsts arranged early in 1941 for their disposal at auction late in that year. The catalogue was printed and distributed well before the sale which took place as scheduled,

December 10, 1941, three days after Pearl Harbor. Though
it was not what the trade calls a slaughter, the books under-
standably brought considerably less than they would have,
had the sale taken place two days before Pearl Harbor. Such
are the fortunes of auction and war.

"If a collector's books are sold to a dealer, the dealer prices
them, advises customers of anything he has picked up which
he knows they are looking for, and puts the rest on his
shelves.

"If they are sold at auction, the auction house has its experts go over the collection and catalogue it. The catalogue,
when printed, describes the books in detail, and accurately—
including condition. A date is set for the sale, the catalogues
are distributed, the books are placed on the shelves for inspection—not many people like to buy anything sight unseen,
and this is and should be particularly true of rare books.

"Now suppose you are getting catalogues regularly and
notice one day that a copy of the 1893 *Maggie* is coming up
for sale. You live outside of New York, and can't conveniently
attend the sale yourself. You can, if you like, submit a bid
direct to the auction house, in which case, if your bid is
high enough, you will get the book at whatever figure the
house has to pay for it to beat the highest opposing bid, and
the house bid may be much lower than the figure you name.
Suppose you submit a bid of two hundred dollars, and
the highest opposing bid is one hundred and thirty dollars,
the bidding proceeding by five-dollar jumps. In that case
you're likely to get your book for one hundred and thirty-five
dollars.

"Suppose, however, that you prefer to have a personal
representative act for you—that is, a rare-book dealer. You
can do one of three things: commission him to bid in the
book for you, naming a price beyond which you don't care
to go; ask him to use his own judgment, withdrawing from
the competition if the bidding runs wild, or tell him to buy

the book for you at all costs. I believe the second plan is the soundest; the dealer should know prices if anyone does, and should protect his client by withdrawing from the bidding as soon as the figure becomes excessive, as it sometimes does.

"Your inability to attend a sale may work to your advantage. A book auction is a public affair. Anyone can come. Dealers, of course, do most of the bidding and most of the buying. They do it calmly, in cold blood, perfectly aware of what it's all about. See a book auction someday when you get a chance. You probably won't be able to tell who's doing the bidding. The turn of a finger, the flip of a catalogue may send the price up at the rate of a hundred dollars a second. I know of one dealer who has an understanding with the auctioneer that he's to be considered in the bidding as long as he carries a pencil behind his ear. I know of plain spectators at book auctions who've nearly contracted paralysis from sitting stock still for two hours because they were afraid a chance move might be interpreted as a bid.

"The dealer is proof against the psychology of the auction room, but the casual spectator, however much he may know about books, is not. Often I've seen a pair of zealots bidding their heads off in a frenzy of competition, boosting the price of a book to a height they both knew was ridiculous, tossing real dollars around as recklessly as if those dollars were just matches in a played-for-fun poker game. Drunk with excitement.

"Now if you have a dealer representing you, and ask him to get into a free-for-all like that, he'll do it—he's a soldier under orders. But don't you see how much better it is to ask him to use his own judgment? In a way it's to his own interest to pay all he can, since he's working on a commission—usually 10 percent. But those commissions aren't going to last very long if he goes throwing his customer's money around promiscuously.

"Here's another and even more important advantage in

letting a dealer represent you. Some auction houses sell every lot without recourse, others allow the return of a lot within a few days if it is not as represented. If the nonprofessional bids in a book, and much later finds it is defective, or even a forgery (not many books are worth forging, considering the expense and skill which forging involves, but the few forgeries that do exist are troublesome), he's just out of luck. If he is represented by a dealer, the dealer will stand squarely behind his judgment—and what he buys and sells. Whatever he sells, whether it comes off his own shelves or is bought for a customer at auction, carries his guarantee. He can do business on no other basis.

"Now suppose you commission a dealer to buy a book for you at what he considers a fair price, how are you going to know that that price won't be excessive? It's to his own immediate and narrow interest, as I've said, to pay all he can for a book at auction, since his commission increases with the cost of the book. Is there any means by which the collector can inform himself of the approximate value of a book which he wants?

"In one sense, no. There is no standard price for a rare book. A rare book—a really rare book—almost invariably changes hands in a seller's market. It is worth whatever an eager buyer wants to pay for it. And because a book sold for fifty dollars five years ago, it does not follow that it will sell for fifty dollars today.

"There are, however, straws to indicate which way the price wind is blowing. I have already mentioned priced auction catalogues. Dealers' catalogues are another good indication. Then there is published, every year, a well-nigh indispensable summary of auction prices called *American Book-Prices Current*, which is compiled from auction catalogues covering the previous season.

"A glance at it will convince you of the truth of what I've

just been saying about prices. Let's find a good example. Here is one: Philip Dormer Stanhope, Lord Chesterfield's *Letters Written to His Son.* This was published in London in 1774 in two volumes, and the edition must have been large, as copies of the first printing are not unusually rare. The value depends entirely upon condition. Four copies are recorded as sold at auction in New York in this volume. One, "original boards, rebacked, no labels," brought $250. A second, "contemporary calf, two hinges cracked, cover defects," $75. A third, "contemporary half calf, hinges cracked, cover defects, marginal stains," $60. And the fourth copy, lacking half-titles, $30.

"Now if someone asked you the value of a first edition of Chesterfield's *Letters,* what would you say? Would you average these four figures? That would give you about a hundred dollars which, like so many averages would be utterly meaningless. Your only accurate answer would be: someone wanted a first enough to pay $250 for a rather poor copy in boards, and someone else wanted one enough to pay $30 for a copy lacking the half-titles. Those facts are indisputable.

"And don't forget the supremely important element of condition. *American Book-Prices Current* gives brief descriptions of defects, but it cannot—nor can any verbal description—give an accurate idea of the exact condition of a given copy of a book. A rare book must be seen to be appreciated—it must also be seen to be depreciated.

"Anyway, arm yourself with a copy of *American Book-Prices Current,* or have your local library buy one if they haven't it already. Study it, study auction and dealers' catalogues, write me or any dealer in whom you have confidence when you want specific information, and you'll be doing all you intelligently can to keep in touch with price developments in the rare-book field."

The dealer pauses and lights another cigarette.

"I'll try to remember all you've told me," says Smith. "And perhaps someday you'll be able to get an 1893 *Maggie* for me."

Perhaps Dealer C will. Perhaps Smith will find one himself. One title he did acquire quickly was the Starrett-Williams revised Crane bibliography, where he learned, among much else, that *The Eternal Patience* may have been a tentative title for *The Third Violet*. Perhaps the quest will be in vain, and Smith be gathered to his fathers without ever having possessed the book. But he will have had the thrill of hoping, of anticipating—the supreme joy of being perpetually on the edge of discovery.

❖   ❖   ❖   ❖

Now all of the above occurred langsyne, and we have been unable to follow Smith's career closely during the turbulent interval. We know that he made it his business for a time to get to New York as often as he could, and that he somehow contrived his affairs to enable him to be in the city while an occasional important auction sale was in progress. Book auctions, he found, were attended largely by professionals and were conducted in full acceptance of that fact. The auctioneer made no effort to wheedle bids; the virtues of successive lots were not orally proclaimed, for they were already spread upon the catalogue; one bid, or one declined to bid, 'twere well it were done quickly, because the only pressure brought to bear at a book auction is against time, and a bid after the hammer's drop, Smith learned, is considered as bad form as an uppercut after the gong.

The exhibitions preceding book auctions, Smith found, were also attended largely by professionals—too largely. The exhibition in advance of a really distinguished collection converts the showrooms of a big auction house into a veritable museum of treasures effectively displayed and meticulously catalogued. And a presale exhibition of books, it appeared, had one superlative advantage over an orthodox museum— every unit might be taken into one's hand and one might pretend, for a moment, that it was one's own. Here, in full polished calf to preserve it from the ravages of the years and the mauling of loveless fingers, Smith was enabled to inspect a copy of *Odes by Mr. Gray (Price One Shilling)*—but not, alas, to Smith—with "The Gift of the Author" neatly inscribed in the upper right-hand corner of the title page.

Any presale exhibition of books is worth attending, and by acquiring the habit of attendance the visitor will be afforded during a single season a view of virtually the whole collecting panorama. It is a postview rather than a preview, but that makes it all the more interesting. For every collection is but the expression of the collector's personality; one studies his accomplishment and builds the man himself back into his books. Here on these shelves and in these cases, one collector's sentimental and intellectual embodiment maintains for a few days its perfected shape.

Smith managed to get his Crane shelves pretty well filled, and he is particularly pleased with his fine copy of *The Red Badge of Courage* which he finally bought for a hundred dollars.

The last we heard of him he was carefully saving against the day when one of the unearthed *Maggies* should come his way. Meanwhile, in order to keep his collecting hand in, he buys an occasional war novel in first edition, and we understand he is compiling a checklist of these. As he reads them too, he is rapidly becoming something of an authority on their contents as well as on their bibliographic niceties.

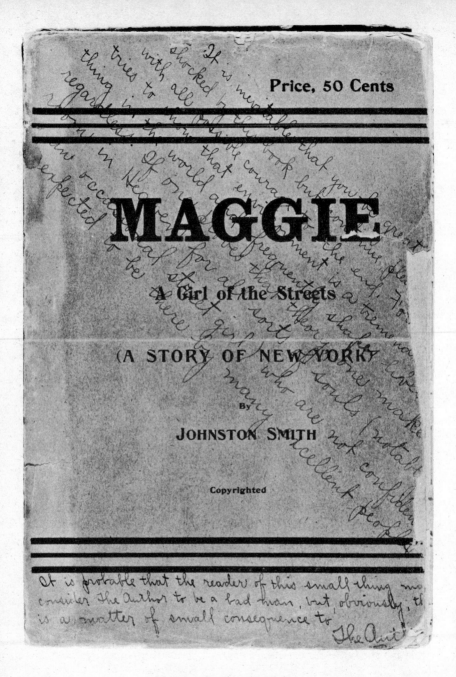

Price, 50 Cents

MAGGIE

A Girl of the Streets

(A STORY OF NEW YORK)

By

JOHNSTON SMITH

Copyrighted

Maggie, Stephen Crane's
first book, a presentation copy.

■

CHAPTER SIX

THE
PURSUIT
OF
THE
POINT

■

The question most frequently put to a book collector by a noncollector is, "How do you tell a first edition?"

The implication is that the collector has some recondite means of identifying a first edition—a divining rod which probes into the mystic past (or present) of print.

The noncollector can see how a tea taster is able to school his senses to detect the excellence or lack of it in the brew before him, how the Oriental rug expert can tell where and when a rug was woven, how the specialist in Japanese prints can identify a Hiroshige at a glance. But—"Why, this is just a book. How do you know it's a first edition?"

As a matter of fact, it is a much simpler problem to identify a first edition than it is to pass judgment on almost anything else that comes within the collector's ken. The tea taster, the rug fancier, the connoisseur of Japanese prints must depend on expert knowledge plus a sixth sense that enables them to know the true from the false. Such a sixth sense comes not amiss to the book collector, but in most instances he has little need to draw on it. It has already been remarked that the problem of forgeries rarely has to be faced in collecting books, for the reason that a book is such a difficult thing to copy that the game of imitating printed rarities for fraud is hardly worth the candle. The career of the late Thomas James Wise, exposed as a forger extraordinary by the two brilliant booksellers John Carter and Graham Pollard in *An Enquiry into the Nature of Certain Nineteenth-Century Pamphlets* (London, 1934) is worth anyone's reading, collector or not. But, generally speaking, the situation is so rarely faced that the question of forgeries, despite its obvious fascination, need have no place in an elementary discussion of book collecting.

The way to identify a first edition is to consult an authority who knows more about it than the consulter. That authority is the bibliographer. Bibliography is the science of describing books.

The primary weapons in the armory of a book collector should be the best available bibliographies of the authors in whom he is interested. To attempt to collect Mark Twain without Merle Johnson, Oscar Wilde without Stuart Mason, Edwin Arlington Robinson without Beecher Hogan, Thomas Wolfe without George Preston, Jr., or Robert Frost without W. B. Shubrick Clymer and Charles R. Green (to cite a few examples among hundreds of available manuals) would be a vain, profitless, and singularly unintelligent pursuit. No bibliography is perfect; some approach perfection much more closely than others. But whatever its shortcomings, a bibliography is likely to be infinitely more reliable than any other source of information available to the collector, some dealers' catalogues alone excepted—and the dealer's cataloguer works with piles of bibliographies at his elbow, and is able to take advantage of the latest available information.

Not every collected author, however, has won the distinction of having a full-dress bibliography of his writings compiled, though of all except the very latest there usually exists somewhere at least a "checklist."

Here the collector's reliance must be such sources as auction and dealers' catalogues, *American Book-Prices Current*, and the data in the files of dealers—data which record the latest and most detailed information. While the dealer naturally does not care to have inquisitive persons going through his files, he will always be glad to inform a customer regarding specific items.

But are there no general rules to be applied in the hunt for books apart from putting full faith in bibliographers and cataloguers? There are a few which can be relied upon, though not invariably. There are books labeled "First edition" which are not first editions at all, either with intent to deceive or by a publisher's oversight, and there are books labeled "Second edition," "Third edition," "Fourth edition," and "Fifth edition" which are authentic first editions—when Thackeray edited *The Snob* (1829) various issues of the publication were so designated in a humorous effort to convey the appearance of a vast circulation. In the face of such a dilemma the collector can hardly be expected to grasp the situation without outside assistance.

Generalities are nowhere so dangerous as in the field of book collecting, but a few, duly qualified, may be ventured:

Unless there is definite indication that a book is not a first edition, it very likely is a first edition. Here is a book designated "Second thousand"—obviously a first thousand preceded it. Here are books labeled "New Edition," "Revised Edition," "New Edition with Illustrations," "New Edition with New Matter" (hence first edition for the "new matter").

Here is a book wherein one reads on the copyright page: "First printing September 1922. Second printing October 1922." In the same place in another book one reads: "Published June 1914. Reprinted August 1914, September 1914 (twice)."

Here is plain evidence that the books so marked are not first editions. Consider, too, such a case as that of Joel Chandler Harris' *Uncle Remus: His Songs and His Sayings* (New York, 1881). Here the only discoverable distinction between first and second issues are the facts that in the second issue the advertisements following text quote from reviews of the book (obviously these could not have appeared until copies of the first issue had become available to reviewers); and the incorrect *presumptive* for *presumptuous* (last line, page 9). Devotees of the dust jacket, however, must be on the alert for authentic first editions which nonetheless carry critical comment of the book itself on the jacket.

The practice of casing review copies in stout wrappers, plain or embellished, is not a phenomenon of recent origin in the history of publishing promotion. The custom may well go back to the infancy of the thundering quarterlies—to the beginnings of book reviewing as it is known today. In an era when the book buyer dressed his purchase to suit his taste, it was not likely that the publisher would waste full calf, or even cloth-backed boards (meaning no offense), on a reviewer. When the London house of T. Werner Laurie issued a facsimile of the Kilmarnock Burns (1786) in 1927, the copies were sheathed in the original (as it were) gray-blue unlettered wrappers, and it is probable that the copies of the original issue sent to the critical great in Edinburgh and London were likewise in wrappers. The custom doubtless prevailed, at least in Great Britain, up to the time cloth bindings became general a century and a half ago.

The wrappered review copy is used today mainly in the

instance of books which publishers and reviewers recognize in advance as of sufficient importance to command the tops of book columns and the front pages of the weekly reviews— and of sufficient importance, too, to be governed by a release date that admits of no *nisi prius*. The publisher, therefore, in order to allow the reviewer all the time he can, dispenses with the elegances of textile investiture.

And thereby another problem is plopped into the collector's lap. "Prefirst editions," these wrappered skirmishers are occasionally called, and the collector shudders at the logic that will admit a prefirst (though French booksellers catalogue a periodical appearance as "édition préoriginale"), because if a prefirst, why not a preprefirst, a pre-times-x first, until one day there may appear in the auction room a ream of white paper on which a collected poet planned to compose a collectable epic when he got around to it?

But the publisher who foresees a collector as well as a general sale for a projected book has devised a neat way out of what in the past has proved a dilemma to publisher, bookseller, collector, and bibliographer. The review copies of a new book by a collected author are likely today to be the first to go out into the world, but they are unlikely to be the first to leave the press. The press, according to the practice of some publishers, will be arbitrarily halted and a "second printing" slug inserted below the copyright notice (a moderately disingenuous proceeding) and copies of this "edition," in wrappers or in definitive boards or cloth, are sent out for review. The practice is not wholly indefensible; at least it meets the ineptitude of the zealous wrappered-copy collector with a neutralizing counterineptitude. However, it must be admitted that some collectors prefer these wrappered review copies and are willing to back their preference with their money. For example, there were one hundred review copies, in plain wrappers, of Thomas Wolfe's

Look Homeward, Angel: the only copy which has appeared at auction came up in the Hogan sale and fetched $200, about five times what the first edition in the first dust wrapper was currently bringing. It's a difference of opinion that makes auction records as well as horse races.

This is the day of the collector of modern firsts (in stating which fact we are casting no slightest aspersion on the collector of the firsts of yesterday and the day before, with whom we feel a closer alliance than with his up-to-date brother), and the collector whose firsts come hot from the press has a distinct advantage. He knows beforehand when a book is to be published and what it is to be, and while the publisher may not broadcast the alteration in plans in composing room or bindery which produces a point, an alert bibliographer or bookseller will soon have the secret ferreted out. Moreover, virtually every publisher now has some means of identifying the sequence of printings—a step taken not so much for the collector's benefit as the publisher's own. In 1928 the late H. S. Boutell had the admirable inspiration to write to publishers in England and the United States requesting data on the keys they employed in identifying impressions and editions. His findings were embodied in a compact, eminently useful summary, *First Editions of Today and How to Tell Them,* which proved so popular that in 1965 a fourth edition, revised and enlarged by Wanda Underhill, was issued. Harper & Brothers, for example, use a code system, the letters A to M representing, in order, the months from January to December (J is omitted, as it is in military designations and also in street identifications in the District of Columbia, and a second letter the year—A for 1926, B for 1927, and so on. Thus a Harper book labeled B—F was published in February, 1931—and if this was the first edition, the words "First Edition" appeared with the label. If the book was reprinted in June, 1932, the new printing would be marked F—G, and "First Edition" would not appear. Houghton Mifflin's practice is to date the title page of the first edition and omit the date on later printings. The Macmillan Company gives month and year of publication below the copyright notice and adds the date of subsequent printings, so that a Macmillan book marked simply "Published May, 1934" is *ipso facto* a first edition. Mr. Boutell's circularization of publishers was itself responsible for influencing many of them who had previously employed no hard-and-fast identifying systems to invent systems by which they have since abided. An example is Scribner's who, late in 1929 (but not early enough to use on *Look Homeward, Angel*), began placing the letter A under the copyright notice of the first edition and removing it thereafter. This has worked well enough except where the printers forgot to put it on at all, which is what happened in the case of Robert Sherwood's *Abe Lincoln in Illinois* (1938).

If there is no prima facie evidence that a book is not a first edition, this test should be applied to it if it was published in America: Are the copyright date and the date on the title page identical? If they are, the book is very likely a first edition. A book might, however, have been copyrighted late in 1881 and not published until 1882 (as in the case of the first edition of Mark Twain's *The Prince and the Pauper*). Again, a book may have been copyrighted in 1889 and have the date 1890 on the title page, as in the second edition of Bret Harte's *The Heritage of Dedlow Marsh*—the first edition is dated 1889, but the 1890 printing has the earmarks of a first edition. When more than a year intervenes between the copyright date and the date of publication, the collector may be virtually positive that the book under consideration is not a first edition. Yet the London 1901 edition of Stephen Crane's *The Monster and Other Stories*, an authentic first edition, carries an 1899 copyright date.

English law, unfortunately, does not require the date after the notice "All rights reserved." Reprints, however, are customarily indicated, and the statement "First published in 1924" on the reverse of the title page can generally be accepted as proof of first edition, barring specific indication to the contrary. But a check should be made with any advertisements at the end of the book, which in many English (and occasionally in older American) books are dated. Here, for instance, is a book designated as "First published in 1907" with thirty pages of advertisements at the back dated July, 1912. This means that in 1912 the publisher bound up sheets of a book printed in 1907 and inserted the latest printing of his catalogue. Conceivably this copy might have been the first off the press in 1907, but hundreds of its brothers were put in circulation (with catalogues dated 1907) five years ahead of it.

Happily for bibliographers, the custom of binding in separate pamphlets of advertisements (as distinguished from advertisements that are a part of the book itself) is no longer practiced in this country. Indeed, only a few American publishers now use advertisements which form part of a signature. Authors may have raised objections. The publishers themselves may have come to look on the practice as slightly undignified. Moreover, the jacket now carries much of the advertising load formerly borne by the book itself.

In an earlier day the vogue of the inserted leaves of advertising matter was so universally prevalent that the book published without them was the exception rather than the rule. It attained the height of complexity during the fifteen years from 1850 to 1865—from the Clay Compromise to Appomattox—and that period, unfortunately for bibliographers, coincides with the great era of productivity of the New England group of authors.

Thoreau's *Walden* provides an excellent illustration of the problems to which the inserted advertisements have given rise. *Walden* was published on August 9, 1854, according to Francis H. Allen's bibliography. The regulation cluster of advertising leaves was bound in at the back, and copies of the book are known with advertising pages dated, respectively, April, May, June, and September, 1854. Mr. Allen declares that the dates "cannot be regarded as of serious importance." Yet the average collector insists on the earlier date, and seems to think that he is being defrauded if a dealer attempts to sell him a copy with May advertisements (or, worse yet, September ones) instead of April. On the other hand, one astute collector is in the market specifically for a copy which has the September advertisements. His theory is this: The first copies of the book issued would be likely to carry the publisher's very latest advertising matter. If and when the supply of these pamphlets ran out, the binder would make shift with any of earlier date that happened to be handy. He would use these up in reverse order of date—June before May, May before April. On this entirely reasonable basis, the collector is right in preferring a *Walden* with September advertisements.

Advertisements apart, every copy of *Walden* of the 1854 issue is like every other, so far as research has been able to determine. Suppose, however, that Thoreau or his printer had detected a serious error early in the printing which was forthwith corrected. The book would then, clearly and unequivocally, be divided into a first and second issue. Yet advertisements of any date might be bound in with the first issue, depending on which pile of sheets the binder happened to lay his hands on. Bibliographical research cannot be expected to determine the casual comings and goings of an employee of a New England bookbinding establishment a century and more ago.

But just as a molecule is divisible into atoms, so may there be divisions within a first edition. The collector, early in his collecting career, will see in auction and dealers' catalogues and in *American Book-Prices Current* such descriptions as "first issue of the first edition" and "first edition, second issue"—he has already noted them in this chapter.

Long arguments have been waged over the definition of the distinction between the terms "edition" and "issue." In practice, however, that distinction is this: A publisher projects a printing of two thousand copies of a new book. These two thousand copies will constitute the first edition. The book goes to press. When perhaps five hundred copies have been printed, an error is detected which, while not sufficiently serious to warrant pulping five hundred copies, is eminently worth correcting as the book goes through press. These first five hundred copies will constitute the first issue of the first edition. If the book ever attains collection prestige, the difference in value between the first issue (one of the five hundred) and the second issue (one of the fifteen hundred) will be considerable. A good example is Stevenson's *Kidnapped*. For years any copy bearing the imprint of the London house of Cassel and the date 1886 was sold as the first edition. Then it was discovered by us that several significant corrections had been made in the text to correct errors, and that there were two distinct issues of the first edition. The first has the following readings: Page 40, line 11, *business*—later *pleasure;* page 64, first line, *nine*—later *twelve;* page 101, line 10, *Islands*—later *Island.*

The order of issue is determined by a letter from Stevenson to his American publisher, Charles Scribner, written from Skerryvore, July 16, 1886, which was recently discovered in the publisher's files:

"Re *Kidnapped,* please note the following corrections which I shall be heartily obliged if you would make at your earliest convenience, as all three are of some importance and have happened from a variety of mishaps. . . ."

Not all books have as definite changes as these, yet they may contain less obvious though just as bibliographically important guides. *Treasure Island*, published in London in 1883, is a case in point. There are several states identifiable by progressive type degeneration. For instance, at some stage in the press run the 8 of the page number 83 dropped out, and the 7 of the page number 127 either dropped out or was replaced by a 7 of an obviously different font. Furthermore, on page 40 of the early press runs the first word of the next to the last line was *miscreant* with a perfect *m* and the first word of the last line was *rain* (for *vain*); in later states the *m* is so broken as to resemble an *n* and the *r* in rain is so smashed as to be unidentifiable. On page 46, line 5, the last word *all* was originally perfect; in later states the last *l* has dropped out; and on page 129 there was a period at the end of the first sentence, missing in later states, etc.

A mark of identification that distinguishes one issue of a first edition from another issue (or from other issues) is called a point. A misprint, broken type, an ornament upside down, a libelous statement later excised or altered, a different color or texture of binding, howlers by the author, the presence or absence of certain illustrations, a different quality of paper, alterations by the author, the presence or absence of tint on the top edges of the sheets or a change in the tints, watermarks, errors in grammar, the color of the endpapers, the lettering on the cover, malicious vulgarity, a change of publishers while the book is being manufactured—this is the stuff that points are made of.

When Mark Twain's *Life on the Mississippi* (Boston, 1883) was first published, the caption to the illustration on page 443 was "The St. Louis Hotel" and on page 441 there was a sketch of Mark being cremated. Later the caption was changed to "The St. Charles Hotel," and the sketch, because Mrs. Clemens objected to it, was removed. The Mark Twain collector will insist on his *Life on the Mississippi*

The suppressed illustration from
Twain's *Life on the Mississippi*.

having both "The St. Louis Hotel" caption and the cremation illustration.

Theodore Dreiser's *A Hoosier Holiday* was originally published at New York in 1916. The date is significant. The First World War was on; America was not yet in it, but close to the edge. On page 173 of the first issue occurs the following passage:

> *We did not stay so long in Buffalo this day, but longer than we would have if we could have discovered at once that Canada had placed a heavy license tax on all cars entering Canada, and that, because of the European War, I presume, we would have to submit to a more thorough and tedious examination of our luggage than ordinarily. The war! The war! They were chasing German-American professors out of Canadian colleges, and making other demonstrations of hostility towards all others having pro-German leanings. I, with my German ancestry on one side and my German name and my German sympathies— what might they not have done to me! We didn't go. In spite of our plans to cross into Canada here and come out at Detroit at the west end of Lake Erie, we listened to words of wisdom and refrained.*

This was a heady brew for 1916. In the second issue the tone of this passage was considerably softened, an altered page was printed, and the sheet tipped in in place of the original sheet (pages 173–174), as is patent on casual inspection. Between the words "ordinarily" and "We didn't go" this makeshift text was inserted, to occupy the same amount of room:

> *Naturally there was much excitement, and on all sides were evidences of preparations being made to send arma- ments and men to the Mother Country. We had looked*

forward with great pleasure to a trip into Canada, but the conditions were so unfavorable that we hesitated to chance it.

The offending leaf thus rudely ripped out is known as a *canceled* leaf, and the leaf that replaces it as a *cancel*. The practice is one that the collector is likely to associate chiefly with books printed no later than the end of the eighteenth century, but cancels occur to this day, although they are resorted to only in serious emergencies. We recall a book of a few years ago (which must be nameless by an agreement made with the compilers in return for this information—it is not a collector's item, so far as we know) which can show all these states in first edition:

First: Serious typographical error, affecting two lines, on page (let us say) 15; leaf with pages 15 and 16 part of signature.

Second: Same as first, save for insertion of errata slip giving correct reading.

Third: Pages 15 and 16 cancelled, and new leaf (cancel) inserted with correct reading (errata slip, of course, omitted).

Fourth: Signature containing pages 15 and 16 reprinted, with error on page 15 corrected.

In this particular instance, it is noteworthy that the page proofs gave the correct reading on page 15; obviously the form was dropped after the final okay, and the linotype slugs pushed back into place (or what was supposed to be place) contrary to orthodox composing-room practice, which demands the re-proving of every form which suffers a comparable accident. And if anyone thinks this incident is utterly lacking in human interest, let it be added that the offending printer may have been fired or at least docked, so that the affair was of more than purely bibliographic interest to him.

In *The Age of Innocence* (New York, 1920) Edith Wharton made the amusing slip (page 186) of having a clergyman inaugurate a wedding ceremony with the opening words of the burial service. This error does not, however, constitute a point, as it persisted through several early printings. Mrs. Wharton seems to have been plagued by such lapses; in *A Son at the Front* (New York, 1923), one character "let her lips droop over her magnificent eyes."

More extensive than the alterations made in Theodore Dreiser's little disquisition on the First World War is the metamorphosis achieved between the first and second issues of Frank Norris's powerful *McTeague* (New York, 1899). The hulking dentist has taken Mrs. Sieppe, her daughter Trina, and her little son Owgooste to the theatre. Thus, in the second issue, page 106:

"Save der brogramme, Trina," whispered Mrs. Sieppe. "Take ut home to popper. Where is der net redicule, eh? Haf you got mein handkerchief, Trina?"

But McTeague was in distress. He had lost his hat. What could have become of it? Again and again he thrust his hand blindly underneath the seat, feeling about upon the dusty floor. His face became scarlet with embarrassment and with the effort of bending his great body in so contracted a space; he bumped his head upon the backs of the seats in front of him.

At length he recovered it from a remote corner, in company with Mrs. Sieppe's reticule, sadly battered by a score of feet. He clapped it upon his head with a breath of relief. But when he turned about to hand her reticule to Mrs. Sieppe he was struck with bewilderment. Neither Mrs. Sieppe, Trina, nor Owgooste was anywhere in sight. McTeague found himself staring into the faces of some dozen people whose progress he was blocking.

"What—where are they gone?" muttered McTeague.

He gazed about him in great embarrassment, rolling his eyes. But the moving audience had carried the Sieppes farther down the aisle. At last McTeague discovered them and crushed his way to them with bull-like force and directness. They, meanwhile, sidled into an empty row of seats to wait for him.

The party filed out at the tail end of the audience.

In the first issue the passage which occupied the identical space had read thus:

"Save der brogramme, Trina," whispered Mrs. Sieppe. "Take ut home to popper. Where is der hat of Owgooste? Haf you got mein handkerchief, Trina?"

But at this moment a dreadful accident happened to Owgooste; his distress reached its climax; his fortitude collapsed. What a misery! It was a veritable catastrophe, deplorable, lamentable, a thing beyond words! For a moment he gazed wildly about him, helpless and petrified with astonishment and terror. Then his grief found utterance, and the closing strains of the orchestra were mingled with a prolonged wail of infinite sadness.

"Owgooste, what is ut?" cried his mother, eyeing him with dawning suspicion; then suddenly, "What haf you done? You haf ruin your new Vauntleroy gostume!" Her face blazed; without more ado she smacked him soundly. Then it was that Owgooste touched the limit of his misery, his unhappiness, his horrible discomfort; his utter wretchedness was complete. He filled the air with his doleful outcries. The more he was smacked and shaken, the louder he wept.

"What—what is the matter?" inquired McTeague.

Trina's face was scarlet. "Nothing, nothing," she exclaimed hastily, looking away. "Come, we must be going. It's about over." The end of the show and the breaking up of the audience tided over the embarrassment of the moment.

The party filed out at the tail end of the audience.

On page 6 of *Our Hundred Days in Europe* (Boston, 1887) Oliver Wendell Holmes wrote:

> *Among the monuments [in Westminster Abbey], one to my namesake Rear Admiral Charles Holmes, a handsome young man, standing by a cannon. He accompanied Wolfe in his expedition which resulted in the capture of Quebec. Dryden has immortalized him, in the "Annus Mirabilis," as "the Achates of the general's fight."*

One of those useful but disturbing creatures who are quick to detect human error in its strictly objective manifestations pointed out to Dr. Holmes that the admiral had pretty nearly immortalized himself without Dryden's assistance, since if he was old enough to receive mention in *Annus Mirabilis,* which was published in 1667, he must have been well on in his second century when he assisted Wolfe at Quebec in 1759. In later issues of *Our Hundred Days in Europe* the anachronism is healed as follows:

> *Among the monuments, one to Rear Admiral Charles Holmes, a descendant, perhaps, of another namesake, immortalized by Dryden in the "Annus Mirabilis" as*
> *"the Achates of the general's fight."*
> *He accompanied Wolfe in his expedition which resulted in the capture of Quebec.*

Not every schoolboy may remember Kwasind, the strong man, and how

> *Straight into the river Kwasind*
> *Plunged as if he were an otter,*
> *Dove as if he were a beaver.*

Kwasind does this, however, only in early copies of the first edition of *The Song of Hiawatha* (Boston, 1855)—page

96, line 7. In subsequent appearances of the poem, he has

Dived as if he were a beaver.

Besides this, the collector's copy must read, page 27, line 9; *heron,* rather than the later *curlew;* page 32, line 11; *In the moon when nights are brightest* which later became *To the melancholy North-Land;* and page 39, line 11: *Wahonomin,* later changed to *Wahonowin.*

The first American book to carry a rhymed title page was James Russell Lowell's *A Fable for Critics* (New York, 1848). It is herewith reproduced in the couplet form in which it is written, with the actual typographical divisions also indicated:

> *Reader! walk up at once (it will soon be too late)*
> *And / buy at a perfectly ruinous rate /*
> *A / Fable for Critics; / or, better, / (I like,*
> *As a thing that the reader's fancy may strike, /*
> *An old-fashioned title-page, / such as presents*
> *A tabular view of the volume's contents) /*
> *A glance / at a few of our literary progenies /*
> *(Mrs. Malaprop's word) / from / the tub of Diogenes; /*
> *A vocal and musical medley. / That is, /*
> *A series of jokes / by a wonderful quiz, /*
> *Who accompanies himself with a rub-a-dub-dub,*
> *Full of spirit and grace, / on the top of the tub. /*
> *Set forth in / October, the 21st day,*
> *In the year '48: / G. P. Putnam, Broadway.*

In the first issue of the book the line "A vocal and musical medley" was omitted, thus scrambling meter and rhyme-scheme alike. An even more amusing contretemps occurred later. The house of Putnam moved to 10 Park Place, and the title page substituted the new address, turning the final couplet into a complete wreck. George Willis Cook's Lowell bibliography quotes a letter of the author, written more than forty years later, in which he stated his belief that the publisher at no time in the book's career noted the fact that the title page was in rhyme. Regarding the substitution of Park Place for Broadway Lowell remarked: "I don't remember whether I knew of it at the time, but had I known, I should have let it pass as adding to the humor of the book." The omitted line, unfortunately, is not the sole distinguishing mark of the first issue of *A Fable for Critics*—that honor apparently belongs to pages 63 and 64 which are misnumbered.

Alterations in the scheme of binding decoration are frequently the means of determining a point. Why the alterations were made is often undeterminable; the obvious fact stands out that they *were* made, and clearly by design, not by accident. Thus, what are supposed to be the very earliest copies of Oliver Wendell Holmes's *The Autocrat of the Breakfast Table* (Boston, 1858) have five little conventional decorations on the backstrip, while inferentially later copies have only four. Actual priority has never been and probably never can be determined, but the publishers certainly never went back to the five-decoration scheme, and copies with the five decorations are rare to such a degree that, for the comfort of all concerned, they are generally regarded as a sort of experimental issue. Generally speaking, a book as relatively common as *The Autocrat of the Breakfast Table* is absolutely ruined by having a leaf torn out. The Hogan copy in the "five-star" binding was sold at his auction for $180 and returned after the sale as defective (lacking pages 263–264). Yet when it was correctly recatalogued with the missing leaf being noted, it still brought $50—more than an ordinary copy in the four-star binding in its condition was currently worth. This was purely because of its rarity. The ear-of-corn decoration on the backstrip of Booth Tarkington's *The Gentleman from Indiana* (New York, 1899) is upside down in some copies, giving it the appearance of an awkward grasshopper about to take off. The earliest copies of Emerson's *Representative Men* (Boston, 1850) have an hourglass design in the middle of the front and back covers. The first issue of Emerson's *Essays* (Boston, 1841) does not carry the designation "First Series" on the backstrip. Here the logic is elementary and unassailable. The collection would hardly be labeled "First Series" unless there were a second series, and *Essays: Second Series* was not issued until 1844, so that copies of the original series which are labeled "First Series" clearly were not bound up until three years after the original appearance of the book.

Change in the kind or grade of paper during the printing process makes a legitimate division into issues. Usually this alteration is to be distinguished by its making the book thinner or thicker. The first issue of James Branch Cabell's *Jurgen* (New York, 1919) measures one and one-quarter inches across the top (including covers), and the first issue of Edgar Lee Masters' *Spoon River Anthology* (New York, 1915) seven-eighths of an inch—later printings are noticeably thicker. Alteration in the paper separating the first two editions of Ernest Hemingway's *Men Without Women* (New York, 1927) is determinable not by thickness but by weight —the first edition of the book weighs slightly more than fifteen ounces, the second between thirteen and fourteen. When this distinction was announced by Hemingway's bibliographer, Louis Henry Cohn, there were audible tongue-cluckings on the part of certain collectors and booksellers, but the point is as honest a one as the removal of the cremation cut and the change in the hotel name in Mark Twain's *Life on the Mississippi.* Moreover, the data was taken directly from the publisher's records and is as unassailable as a geometric axiom.

There are collector's items to which one might devote a lifetime of careful study without being able to determine, beyond the peradventure of a doubt, all the precise points of a first issue. The "twenty parts in nineteen" in which *The Posthumous Papers of the Pickwick Club* (London, 1836–1837) was first issued require eighty-five pages to collate in Thomas Hatton and Arthur H. Cleaver's *A Bibliography of the Periodical Works of Charles Dickens, Bibliographical, Analytical and Statistical* (London, 1933). Each part is subjected to an elaborate analysis of wrappers, advertisements, plates, and text; and even so there are some matters still unsolved. Certain *Pickwick* points are, however, indisputable. The plates in Part III must be by R. W. Buss. These, known as the "suppressed plates," were five months later replaced by two others designed and etched by "Phiz." "Phiz" himself, however, created a point when in the last part he inscribed a sign "Tony Veller" instead of "Tony Weller." The rarest of all the plates in *Pickwick* are the two in Part VI, Nos. XIV and XV having the incorrect pagination (pages 169 and 154 reversed). The error must have been quickly detected and the correction made before many impressions were run off. The artist immediately etched over the original figures and gave the pages their proper numbers. These are just a few of the points which make the acquisition of a "perfect *Pickwick* in parts," i.e., one which may be designated as 100 percent perfect, somewhat more difficult for a rich man than entering into the Kingdom of Heaven.

The "Veller" error is not the only Dickens mixup made by "Phiz." Plate 29 in Part 15 of *Nicholas Nickleby* (London, 1838–1839) comes with two inscriptions, the first long: "Nicholas makes his first visit to the lodgings of Mr. Bray"; and the second short: "Nicholas makes his first visit to Mr. Bray." In the vignette title to *The Life and Adventures of*

Martin Chuzzlewit (London, 1843–1844) appears a signpost which reads "100 £ Reward," signed "Phiz fecit," with seven studs in the lid of Pinch's trunk; or reads "£100 Reward," signed "Phiz," with six studs in lid of trunk; or "£100 Reward," signed "Phiz," with five studs in lid of trunk. In *Dombey and Son* (London, 1846–1848) "Phiz" put Captain Cuttle's hook on the left arm; Dickens erred with him, however, twice referring to Mr. Toots's boat as the *Delight* instead of the *Joy*—to both the delight and joy of subsequent owners of a first issue of *Dombey and Son*.

No such exhaustive research has been done on the tangled bibliography of *Vanity Fair* (London, 1847–1848). Two points are generally noted by auction houses and booksellers in describing "first issues": the misprint "Mr. Pitt," later changed to "Sir Pitt," Part XV, page 453, and the presence of the woodcut on page 336, Part XI, depicting the Marquis of Steyne. The first is no point at all as the change was not made until after all of the first edition had been issued. The woodcut is another matter. The Marquis of Steyne was a fictitious character, but the Marquis of Hertford was not, and the latter objected so strenuously to the portrait on the ground that it resembled him that it was removed. The resemblance was no accident on the part of the author-illustrator.

Only recently, strangely enough, has there been a competently edited edition of *Vanity Fair* or even a reasonably satisfactory bibliographical description of the first edition. One shall not be attempted here. But the collector in considering a copy should make sure of (among scores of other variant readings) the following textual points: Page 29 should have nineteen lines of text, not twenty (this point is vital); page 58, line 7 from bottom, should read *Shiverly Square,* not *Gaunt Square*; page 75, line 29, *Muttondown's,* not *Southdown's*; page 101, last line, "sang to Heaven," not "sang *Te Deum*"; page 152, line 36, *kind heart,* not *sad heart*; page 254, line 9, *shall,* not *shawl*; page 579, lines 7–8, "certain debts and the insurance of his life," not "certain outstanding debts and liabilities," etc.

What research we have done on *Vanity Fair* leads us to prefer copies with the fifth line of the printed title page reading: "With Illustrations On Steel And Wood By The Author," not "With Illustrations on Wood And Steel By The Author"; and with the dedication leaf set in small type (the last line measuring 2 1/8 inches in length), not in larger type (the last line measuring 2 9/16 inches in length). Furthermore, if we were to own a *Vanity Fair* (which we do not), we would be happier with a set having the last four parts dated at the foot of the wrapper than with an undated one; and we would insist on the final double part, XIX–XX, having the wrapper with the name "Thos. Murray" and not "T. Murray" in the imprint.

Sir William Schwenk Gilbert's *The Mikado; or The Town of Titipu* (1885) has a nice point in the first issue of the libretto, which is quite an uncommon book. Yum-Yum's song, "The sun whose rays," appears in the first act, at pages 14–15. As told in the *Gilbert and Sullivan Journal* for October, 1926, Miss Leonora Brahum, who created the part of Yum-Yum, found herself on the opening night so breathless after the gyrations of the "Three little maids from school" that she begged Gilbert to put the song somewhere else, which he promptly did; in all later issues the song appears at page 36.

How is a point discovered? Usually only after the most painstaking and detailed research—involving, perhaps, thorough readings of many different copies of an assumed first edition. "In search of information," declares Mr. Johnson in the introduction to his Mark Twain bibliography, "I have examined almost every available source: libraries, private collections, and have interviewed numbers of publishers, printers, and book dealers." These few modest words summarize years of meticulous effort.

Collector and bookseller live in perpetual terror of the point—the Omarian hair that divides the false and true, that distinguishes the desirable first state of a book from the despicable second. Often the point is utterly pointless—he may have been a cynical bookman who christened a moderate protuberance from the Connecticut shore Point No Point. Often the supposititious point is no more—indeed far less—provable than the priority of the hen or the egg, but somehow it gets itself inscribed on the bibliophilic tablets of the law, and thereafter not even the Supreme Court can budge it. (Suggestion: Why not an actual test case—a friendly, but not too friendly, suit of bookseller versus bibliographer?) The late George H. Sargent pleaded in the first number of the *Colophon* for a true supreme court of bibliography, and everybody said it would be a wonderful thing, but nobody did anything about it, and nobody ever will.

But there is a ray of hope in the point situation—purely adventitious, but none the less a ray. It does not shine forth from the very sun of truth, but at any rate it is luminous, and perhaps one should not inquire too closely into the source of one's light—let the end justify the beams.

Ours is an unregenerate day. Authors, editors, proofreaders err as much as they ever did, but the errors, unless they carry the taint of potential litigation, are often allowed to persist through printing after printing. Not many years ago there appeared a novel by a collected author in which a tennis player attained the ingenious score of twenty love— the player was executed at the end of the second volume, but the author was not even indicted. The error was common to the "trade" and the large-paper limited signed editions, for this novel was born in a day when virtually everything between covers enjoyed such a dual and dubious personality. "Twenty love" persisted through several early printings despite public protest, and may be confounding readers in the most recent—one lacks the heart to investigate these matters too thoroughly. And in the twenty-sixth printing of a novel whose popularity seems proved by that figure, a casual inspector reports two allusions to *McGuffy* readers, *cher amie* (deliberately juxtaposed with *cher ami*), *it's* for *its,* and *Missouri* with a lower-case *m.* Any one of these gaucheries was inexcusable in the first printing—they are rather more than twenty-six times less excusable in the twenty-sixth. Has the cost of stereotyping risen to such appalling heights that replating is not to be considered? Or do publishers (and perhaps authors) just decline to give a damn? Anyway it is all very pleasant for the collector and seller of first editions, for as long as errors stay in, points stay out.

But some errors are so heinous that self-respecting publishers can neither understand how they occurred nor allow them to remain uncorrected. When Scribner's issued Genevieve Foster's *George Washington's World,* it was immediately pointed out to embarrassed publisher and author-illustrator that the map of the Thirteen Original Colonies, page 4, *included* Maine and *excluded* New Hampshire! Until then the classic historical boner we knew about had been committed by the Oxford University Press, which issued in 1925 an illustrated edition of D. H. Lawrence's *Movements in European History.* One of the illustrations (opposite page 270) had the caption: "Washington Street, Boston, showing the Old South Church (still standing). This was the church in which Patrick Henry made his 'Give me Liberty or give me Death' speech." Both publishers acted with commendable zeal in suppressing the errors, recalling copies, canceling plates, etc., but a few copies of each title escaped them, and occasionally appear on the market.

A particularly vicious circle, one hopes, has been constructed in the Inferno for the entertainment of persons who have taken the inept pains to underscore bibliographic points. Notations of any sort in books (unless, of course, they are the work of a distinguished hand) are distressing but often pardonable; after all, anyone who owns a book has a legal, even a moral right to disfigure it as he will, certainly if the disfigurements have some critical or referential value to the marker. Such markings are, obviously, often the work of a tolerably inferior intelligence; there are those who cannot read between the lines without writing between the lines.

It is notable that the most casual marginal criticism is definitely destructive, consisting of heavily etched exclamation points of violent disapproval, eyebrow-elevating question marks, or capitalized NO's. These, of course, are not so hideous as underscorings, which are uniformly delineated with extrablack pencils—uniformly, that is, except where they are done in ink. Underscorings are at least in the main constructive comment, and are patently employed, in most instances, to mark a passage held worthy to be resavored. When the underscoring happens to be in a copy of Emerson's *Essays* of 1841 the business is deplorable but nevertheless defensible, for the underscorer, obviously ignorant of the economic havoc he was raising, was certainly sincere in his eagerness to learn something about Emerson, while the collector may limit his internal examination to a search for foxings.

But there is no defense to be put forward on behalf of the vandal who sets a cross beside the word *dove* on page 96 of *Hiawatha*, or *reduplicate* on page 21 of *The Scarlet Letter*, or the two *so prettys* on page 145 of *The Gentleman from Indiana*. If the marker knows that these affairs are of dollars-and-cents significance, then he knows as well that the disfigurements he makes impair the value of the book. For these pages assume a bibliographical and commercial value equal to that of the title page. It is to them that the casual hand will oftenest turn; it is their edges that will first fray and tear; it is the signature of which they are a part which will be sprung before any of the others. Toss a copy of Mark Twain's *Life on the Mississippi* into the air (but not, please, in a book collector's presence) and it will come down open at page 441 or 443. Why shouldn't it? No one picks it up without looking to see whether it has the cremation cut and the incorrect hotel caption.

Who puts crosses beside *dove* and underscores *reduplicate* anyway? Booksellers? Incredible. Collectors? Equally incredible. Whoever is responsible, it is clearly someone who ought to know better.

The collector must not regard every misprint, every solecism, every instance of defective type as a point until it has been proved guilty. Indeed, if he discovers one book that represents perfection in these concerns he will deserve better of humanity than if he had brought to light a thousand points dividing a thousand first editions of classic works of English and American literature into first issues and second issues. Moreover he will not scorn second issues merely because they are second issues—he will, in fact, do well to equip himself with both first and second issues of every first edition he seeks which is thus divisible.

The collector should be aware of the fact that mechanical collating devices, such as the Hineman machine, have invaded our increasingly automated society. (To collate a book is to give it a thorough physical examination—to see if all the pages are there, both text and illustrations, if any.) The mechanical collator unquestionably has its uses, although to date it seems to have been largely devoted to turning molehills into yet smaller molehills. Perhaps we are unduly prejudiced in favor of the human eye. And, probably, as Pope describes vice: it

> *. . . is a monster of so frightful mien*
> *As, to be hated, needs but to be seen;*
> *Yet seen too oft, familiar with her face,*
> *We first endure, then pity, then embrace.*

To us the collating machine is on a par with the autoclave. Medieval scribes probably felt the same way on first getting a glimpse of Gutenberg's monster.

■

CHAPTER SEVEN

DOLLARS AND CENTS

■

There are benefits which money cannot buy, but Gutenberg Bibles, First Folio Shakespeares, and *Pickwicks* in parts are not among them. It would be the smuggest sort of Pollyannaism to suggest that the poor collector ought to grow rapturous at the spectacle of worthy affluents picking up choice morsels of this class, giving them splendid shelter, and eventually turning them over to the municipality for an uncomprehending public to gape at under glass cases. Book collecting is essentially a selfish pursuit, and the man or woman who collects books on that matter-of-fact basis ought to get the most fun out of the business. In a day when, however wretchedly it may be practiced, the principle of the Golden Rule is preached as never so vehemently before, let us be grateful that at least one oasis of self-interest remains wherein the individual of some cultivation and less ready cash may partake of intellectual sustenance without even having to yield up the core to a fainting fellow creature.

The selfish pleasures of book collecting are of two kinds—

the gratification of possession and the gratification of exhibition. One type of collector is satisfied merely to own, to fondle his treasures in the presence of no other eye, whether that other eye might be the kind that would kindle with reciprocal enthusiasm, or the kind that would grow dull with the glaze of boredom. The other type must continually have his treasures on display, and be never so happy as when expounding to an auditor the delectable trove of a mashed letter *i* or the glory of a missing comma. The hermit and the missionary—these are the two kinds of collectors, and we venture the opinion that the closer the collector's income draws toward zero, the more likely is he to belong in the first classification.

This is no place—if such a place exists anywhere—wherein to present elaborate compilations of the percentages of earnings which sundry groups of humanity should devote to books, old or new, rare or superabundant. That is humanity's own business. Conscience may be called upon if desired, or triumphantly suppressed. If conscience be called upon, a reasonably astute master thereof should be able to override it with a single stupendous argument—to wit, that rare books are a good investment.

Augustine Birrell, essayist and statesman, spoke the simple truth when he wrote (in 1892): "Lower prices are not to be looked for. The book-buyer of 1900 will be glad to buy at today's prices. I take pleasure in thinking he will not be able to do so. These high prices tell their own tale and force upon us the conviction that there never were so many private libraries in course of growth as there are today.

"Libraries are not made; they grow. Your first two thousand volumes present no difficulty and cost astonishingly little money. . . . But pride is still out of the question. To be proud of having two thousand books would be absurd. You might as well be proud of having two topcoats. After your first two thousand difficulty begins, but until you have ten thousand volumes the less you say about your library the better. *Then* you may begin to talk."

This is the same Augustine Birrell who also wrote: "The late Mark Pattison, who had 16,000 volumes, and whose lightest word has therefore weight, once stated that he had been informed, and verily believed, that there were men in his own University of Oxford who, being in uncontrolled possession of annual incomes of not less than £500, thought they were doing the thing handsomely if they expended £50 a year upon their libraries. But we are not bound to believe this unless we like. There was a touch of morosity about the late Rector of Lincoln which led him to take gloomy views of men, particularly Oxford men."

The statement that rare books are a good investment, once baldly ventured, requires amplification, elucidation, and, it must be admitted, considerable hedging on the part of the venturer. We should not advise, nor, we think, would any conscientious rare-book dealer advise, a man with fifty thousand dollars to put it all in first editions of Elizabethan dramatists (not that he could get many) rather than in securities enjoying an AAA rating. Any sound financial adviser will say that the main considerations of an investment are safety of principal and assurance of income, and that a man who looks first to the increase of his principal is a speculator, whether he put his money in Hot Stuff Oil or obligations of the United States Government.

First editions of Elizabethan dramatists cannot, in the very nature of the case, return an income. They are a frozen investment. They are not, in the sense just interpreted, an investment at all—*if* the collector regards them solely as so much property that can at any time be reconverted into cash, and more cash than he paid for them; if, in other words, the owner himself, by regarding increase in the value of his principal as a primary consideration, places them thereby in the category of speculative assets.

This seems to give the lie to the statement, just categorically made, that rare books are a good investment. Example being necessary to precept, let us consider the cases of two men, A and B, both book lovers, both the owners of modest homes and modest libraries.

A cares nothing for books as collector's items. His library comprises in the main well-printed sets of standard authors, standard reference books, and a few feet of volumes given to subjects in which he has a special and intelligent interest (gardening, advertising, banking, sundials, crime, and the naval development of the United States), his surviving college textbooks, an assortment of paperback novels which he has acquired casually from time to time, and a miscellany of secondhand pickups which have chanced to catch his eye. A good proportion of these books are first editions, but not (with a half dozen haphazard exceptions) first editions of any value as such. The whole library may number five or six hundred volumes.

B, on the other hand, has for a dozen years been an earnest and painstaking collector. His library does not lack essential works of reference, and there is a good quantity of casual ephemera that B would be the first person in the world to characterize as trash. There are some standard sets, but B has preferred, wherever possible, to collect sets of first editions—his Emerson shelf is imposing in its width, and represents, with the exception of one or two items, a smaller cash outlay than does the sumptuous half-levant array of Emerson on A's shelves; and it would be difficult for a millionaire starting from scratch to duplicate his Mark Twains and Stevensons (some conspicuous gaps in the latter). B gets a perpetual thrill out of the *Moby-Dick* he bought for twenty dollars many years back). There are some Kelmscotts which

B acquired before the glamour of newness had quite worn off, an engrossing collection of books that were once the property of Presidents (engrossing even if Washington and Lincoln are not among the number), and a few excellent examples of the work of early American printers, including a couple of Franklin imprints. B's library, volume for volume, is about as large as A's.

It is not altogether essential to slaughter our heroes; one might as conveniently have them suffer severe financial reverses, or be suddenly transferred to the Rangoon offices of their respective firms, and so forced to dispose of their books. But the dispersal of B's collection would be a deathblow anyway. So let B be gathered to his fathers, the Groliers of Valhalla, without suffering the spectacle of his collection neatly disposed in packing cases, and for convenience let A perish with him.

A's executors, who have a good eye to bonds, real property, and, with reservations, to antique furniture, are stumped by the books. Rather, instead of being stumped, they regard the books as so much baggage to be got out of the way with all possible expedition. A secondhand dealer is called in, and, somewhat to the surprise of heirs and executors alike, is foolish enough to make a cash offer for the library instead of demanding a premium to cart it away. That offer, however, is about one-tenth of what the books cost A. But everybody is content—especially the secondhand dealer, who has discovered half a dozen first editions that had long blushed unseen on A's shelves for which any rare-book dealer will pay the secondhand dealer as much as the secondhand dealer has spent for the whole library, giving him a margin of some six hundred books' clear profit.

B's executors likewise have an eye to first mortgages and good suburban acreage. They, too, incline to classify books as junk. But B has provided for such a contingency. In his will he has specified that his library is to be inspected by a friendly rare-book dealer from whom he has made many purchases, that the dealer is to buy what he wants at his own price (which B, having confidence in the dealer's integrity, knew would be a fair one), that any books of value which the dealer does not want, he is to dispose of at auction for the benefit of B's estate, and that the remainder—trash, perhaps, from the collector's point of view—are to be trundled off to the secondhand dealer. What is the result? B's library, combining the proceeds of the three methods of disposal, brings more than he paid for it.

Parenthetically it might be noted that dealers of integrity far outnumber those of dubious honesty—scoundrels exist even in the ministry, Sinclair Lewis informs us. And if the collector cannot find a dealer in whose complete honesty and judgment he can place as much faith as he does, say, in that of his doctor or his lawyer, he had better stop collecting. For neither he nor the dealer will have any fun. Collecting is a two-way street, and the rare-book dealer of integrity who feels that a particular collector does not have faith in him (despite, perhaps, an occasional unwitting error) will cheerfully give up that collector.

The weakness of a hypothetical case is that the hypothecator can distort it as he will to gain his ends. This is, we believe, what Mark Twain meant when he said that there are lies, damned lies, and statistics. A statistical analysis can easily be given to show the enormous increase in price during the past thirty years of John J. Audubon's original issue of his four-volume, elephant folio, *Birds of America* (London, Printed for the Author, 1827–1838), and auction records quoted to prove it: 1935, $5,200; 1936, $6,600; 1939, $11,700; 1942, $15,600; 1950, £7,000; 1954, £9,200; 1959, £13,000, and 1962, £4,200 for the first volume *only*.

But again, one could compare the prices (not necessarily

the values) of the books of a dozen other authors temporarily or permanently out of collecting favor to prove that anyone who had seriously collected them on an investment basis a decade ago should have had his head (if any) examined. Consider, for instance, the low esteem in which collectors of today hold Galsworthy, Barrie, Kipling, all gods in decades past. Perhaps one day authors in this group will again enjoy their past popularity. It has happened. But it didn't happen to Andrew Lang, whose multitudinous books (verse, essays, folklore, fairy tales, biography, history) were avidly sought and bought around the turn of the century. Lang himself, who enjoyed the title of "the greatest book-man of his age," provided the perfect example of how not to collect—and did it in his own words.

"We are to be occupied, not so much with literature as with books, not so much with criticism as with bibliography, the quaint *duenna* of literature, a study apparently dry, but not without its humours." So Andrew Lang wrote on the threshold of his book about book collecting, *The Library* (1881), calling the first chapter "An Apology for the Book-Hunter." Though Lang himself collected books, he cannot rank among the great collectors; in book hunting as in other things he was, as Oscar Wilde called him, "the divine amateur." He had neither the money nor the patience to collect either rare books as such or even to wait until he could find perfect copies of the books that he actually wanted. "When I collected books," he wrote in the preface to the second edition of *The Library* (1892), "I got together a wonderful heap of volumes, hopelessly imperfect"; and he advises the true book collector that "it is far wiser to buy seldom, and at a high price, than to run round the stalls collecting two-penny treasures. This counsel was not taken by him who gives it." And further in "Bibliomania" (an article that appeared first in *The Cornhill Magazine*, July, 1902, and was later printed privately in pamphlet form for Paul Lemperly of Lakewood, Ohio, in 1914) he concludes that "the person who, in the first place, wants to *read* his books for pleasure or for purposes of history is hardly a collector at all."

Remember that if book collecting were an easy way to wealth, all book dealers, having an inside track while their collectors have to devote a bit of time to business to earn money to buy books, would have retired long ago. But no. Somehow they hang on, worrying about the rent and whether the next catalogue will gross enough to pay printing costs. On the other hand, very few seem to have starved to death, and even fewer, having once chanced into their fascinating profession, have renounced it.

And the sheer pleasure of possession by the collector must not be overlooked—it cannot be measured by any dollars-and-sense standard. If collector B happened to purchase a first edition, say, of *Moby-Dick* for *x* dollars and it was sold years later for *x* minus, that is not a loss if he had fun and pleasure and pride from its possession while he owned it. And our set buyer, A, did not, we maintain, get that enjoyment from his merchandise. Also, without statistics, we maintain B's possessions will find a more ready market than A's when that unhappy time comes that they must be dispersed.

"All very well," replies some latter-day exemplar of the Clerk of Oxenford. "I should be most happy to collect books as a cultural diversion, and while I should regard the collecting of books for investment as altogether a separate enterprise, I should be happy to know that my books, a generation hence, would be worth two or three or thirty times what I paid for them. It is pleasant to think that Mr. Melville's *Moby-Dick* is today worth far more than a copy could have been picked up for fifty years ago. All very well—for the man who has a few hundred dollars to spend for a single book. I haven't."

This wholly reasonable objection can be met by citing an encouraging example which has the advantage of being true: There is a man who holds a white-collar job, earning thereat rather less than the contemporary carpenter or mason. He is a person of taste and cultivation, an intelligent and discriminating, but nonprofessional, critic. For twenty years he has been buying books—first editions, but he has been buying them as new books, making his own forecast of the judgment which time would make of their authors. He has made few erroneous decisions—and so many accurate ones that we know of at least one dealer who would be glad to pay him a handsome sum for his collection—possibly not a sum that would make a Rothschild jealous, but one that would astonish those of the collector's associates who know him only as an unobtrusive small-salaried creature with a taste for reading.

Anyone who began to acquire, as new books, all the first editions of James Stephens, James Joyce, J. M. Synge, W. H. Hudson, Katherine Mansfield, Edna St. Vincent Millay, Max Beerbohm, Joseph Conrad, Norman Douglas, Mary Webb, and E. M. Forster has no cause to deprecate the soundness of his critical acumen. Yet nearly all of the books of these writers when new sold for no more than two dollars apiece. A man who backed his opinions on George Bernard Shaw, J. M. Barrie, John Steinbeck, Ernest Hemingway, Willa Cather, William Faulkner, and Thomas Wolfe will have no difficulty in getting his money back, and several items by authors in this group will return him fiftyfold. He would, at least, be far ahead of anyone spending the same money who bought only reprints.

Lest the reader jump to the not illogical conclusion that the road to fortune lies in having a small supply of ready cash and employing it in a few judicious purchases of new first editions, it is essential to cite a few instances of time-tried first editions which, for one reason or another, sell at low prices or which once sold well above what they can be purchased for at present—in some instances less than the original retail figure. Several dozen Bret Harte titles are to be had at five dollars each and less, *Mliss* and *The Pliocene Skull* not among them. Many first editions of Thomas Bailey Aldrich, Eugene Field, Joel Chandler Harris, and a host of others of equal or greater repute sell for from one to five dollars apiece—prices that must be a keen disappointment to the speculator. But there are books by most of the authors cited that sell at a heavy premium.

There are two main reasons for the low price of hundreds of collectible first editions: the fact that the low-price books are abundant, and the fact that the authors in question, apart from their scarcer writings, are not, with one or two exceptions, in great present demand. These two reasons may be combined in one: more of these cheap books are in existence than there are collectors who want them. Once the number of collectors begins to approach the supply of available books—and such a condition might come to pass overnight—an immediate bull market will follow.

In the late twenties and early thirties Galsworthy firsts, especially his four first books written under the pseudonym John Sinjohn: *From the Four Winds* (London, 1897); *Jocelyn* (London, 1898); *Villa Rubein* (London, 1900); and *A Man of Devon* (London, 1901) brought many times what they can be purchased for now. The same is true of firsts of Bernard Shaw and numerous others. These books were never genuinely scarce, but there was such a rush of "new money" collectors in those days, all of whom had at least heard of Galsworthy even though they had never read him, that temporarily the demand exceeded the supply, and prices soared accordingly. A good rule of thumb for the beginning collector is never to begin collecting a contemporary author whose books seem inordinately high-priced and popular. Begin with someone less sought after, if you happen to like him, and with patience and luck the others will come along later. And, conversely, do not now completely neglect say Galsworthy or Conrad simply because they are currently selling much below what they brought in 1929. If you like them and believe in their lasting literary qualities, the time of their temporary eclipse is exactly the time to collect them.

Though they may be the despair of the speculator, low-price books are the great opportunity of the collector of small means. Just as the occasional fisherman gets as keen a thrill from landing an unprotesting perch as the big-game hunter derives from bagging his thirty-ninth lion, so will the small book collector gain as much pleasure in the pursuit of the one- and two-dollar items as the millionaire gets in seeking another Caxton. There is another good reason for beginning with small fry. The collector learns about collecting by collecting; playing with inexpensive books, he will become bookwise more quickly than by any other process of education.

Nor need he begin his course in the school of collecting experience by devoting himself wholly to writers of an earlier generation who are long past the heyday of their collecting period or have not yet swum into the collector's ken. There are thirty or more Arnold Bennett first editions (not including, unfortunately, *The Old Wives' Tale* of 1908) which are dear at more than the price of a current novel. Ten dollars invested in G. K. Chesterton can be stretched to cover three or four of his first editions—and three or four volumes is not a bad flying start for any collection.

Is it essential that the collector ultimately acquire the expensive items? That all depends on his personal definition of the word "essential." But this much may be said: half a dozen Mark Twain first editions constitute a collection as certainly as do fifty. The true enthusiast will not want to stop at half a dozen, to be sure; his goal, however visionary it may be rendered by the dimensions of his pocketbook or the sheer practical handicap of attempting to gain what cannot be had, is completeness. But compare for a moment the book collector with the stamp collector. The stamp collector embalms his finds in a convenient album which is cut up into small plots exactly like a real-estate development project, with a stamp assigned to every plot. It matters not how difficult a stamp may be to procure; space is left for it just the same. And as the commoner, then the less common, then the scarce, the rare, and the very rare dabs of neatly engraved parallelograms are convoyed to their appointed havens, the more glaring become the white spots that must remain forever unfilled and unfillable. To deride another's hobby is among the lowest forms of poor sportsmanship—we are not attacking stamp collecting, but the manner in which stamp albums are edited, while conceding that that manner is the relentlessly logical one.

Fortunately books do not have to be assembled into collections in such a perfervidly systematic fashion. Indeed, a book collector is likely to allow considerable latitude to his definition of such an uncompromising and clear-cut term as complete. Completeness, he will often argue, need not mean absolute utter life-and-death completeness. A set of Mark Twain, he will tell you, may reasonably be called complete, though lacking certain slight but perhaps expensive items, provided it contains such an essential as *The Adventures of Tom Sawyer*. Another instance of sour grapes? Perhaps.

Now this argument may sound like the ancient and ideal philosophical discussion as to how many beans constitute a heap, but it has a very direct bearing on the question of dollars and cents. Shall a collector, for instance, confine himself to one or two or three authors, seeking the will-o'-the-wisp completeness, or shall he select a few representative first editions of twenty or thirty authors? In the one case he may have to spend twenty times as much money as in the other. Or he may collect by periods, avoiding the expensive elect, or choosing from their works those whose acquisition will not fling him into involuntary bankruptcy. If he is not a stickler for condition, he can own books which, "as new," he could not hope to afford, but we do not advise this dubious form of economy. Better a few books in the best obtainable condition than a thousand in tatterdemalion, both from the point of view of the satisfaction which they give the possessor and of their resale value.

Again that question of the rare book as an investment! This point has been so heavily stressed in the present chapter that we feel it only an act of justice to the new (or old) collector to let him have the opportunity of hearing a voice in rebuttal. We quote from the foreword to Mr. Milton Waldman's engrossing monograph *Americana: The Literature of American History*.

> *A word about prices. Price is a question that inevitably crops up where rare books are discussed, and I fancy that they interest the public no less than the collector. Hence I give them frequently, but with the distinct understanding that they are not there for the purpose of airing my belief that rare books are a good investment. One hears a great deal about books purchased for ten dollars and sold for a thousand. There are such cases, but they are altogether exceptional, and signify nothing. A Shakespeare first folio, bought in 1623 for perhaps ten dollars, might bring $30,000 today [Mr. Waldman's book was published in 1925] if in first-class condition. But that same ten dollars, if invested at five percent and interest compounded, would now be worth over $300,000,000. Allowing for any possible discrepancy in my calculations, the point is suf-*

ficiently clear to expose the investment fallacy. When I cite the rapid increase in the value of certain books, it is merely because such increases are the arresting exception, not the rule.

We should not urge on anyone the purchase of a First Folio for $30,000 or $100,000, a more realistic figure today—or even $10—on the theory that it might sell for a fabulous figure in the year 2266—one's obligations to posterity can hardly be expected to extend to the twelfth generation. Furthermore, there are scores of books that were published in and around 1623 that are worth no more today than they were as new books, so that the book buyer of 1623 might conceivably have done worse than acquire a First Folio.

A man who considers books primarily as investments or speculations is not a collector. He is in the book business. Now the book business is as honorable a calling as that of a librarian, but a book dealer is not a book collector. He is, in fact, at the very opposite pole. He buys not to hoard, but to dispose of what he buys, and without waiting for a buoyant market. No man can serve two masters, and no wise man tries.

The theory that rare books are a "good investment" is quite as capable of being overworked as is the theory that exercise benefits both man and beast. The library that is built up exclusively as an investment generally proves, when put to the unsentimental proof of the auction room, to contain a sizable fraction of nonmarketable misfits. One reason for this condition is the fact that the collector-for-investment is often misled by the increase in valuation over published price into the belief that, if *Pickwicks* and *Vanity Fairs* published at a shilling a part are today worth many thousand dollars, a book which cost many pounds in its own day (particularly if that day were a century or more ago) must be of impressive value. The theory does not always work out. The India paper issue of Sir Walter Scott's *Border Antiquities of England and Scotland*, for instance, published in two volumes at London in 1813, was issued to sell at the impressive figure of twenty-six pounds fifteen shillings—about $140. The reader is invited to compute for himself the total which would have resulted if a contemplating purchaser of *Border Antiquities* had foregone that luxury and put his money into consols for the benefit of posterity. The book, unfortunately, is not now worth anything like that figure, whatever it might be. A New York shop recently offered an excellent copy for $30. It is, obviously, an item to appeal not to the "investor," but to a person interested in Sir Walter Scott, the history of engraving, or border antiquities.

Acquisition by the New York Public Library of the Tikyll Psalter, which brought the highest price—$61,000—at the sale of selections from the library of the Marquess of Lothian, emphasized anew the inevitable operation of that rider to the law of gravitation whereby every important example of literary or artistic property is destined one day to inclusion in an institutional collection. The worth of a public or semi-public library (assuming as a premise that its contents make it worthy to be called a library) is in pretty direct ratio to its accessibility, and it is eminently fitting that the handiwork of John Tikyll should find a haven at one of the busiest corners in the world, where today's and tomorrow's passing millions can pause to pay it the tribute of reverent inspection. In its new house of refuge the Tikyll Psalter is being carefully tended during whatever approximation to eternity awaits it. It is as durably fabricated as the library building itself, and already has an advantage in seasoning of some six hundred years over the roof that shelters it.

Not every collector can aspire to the *ad interim* custodianship of a Tikyll Psalter, but even though he rotates in a more restricted orbit, he can still apply the institutional test to his collecting activities. "Will this book," he can ask himself, "one day be worthy of inclusion in a public collection, appealing to however numerous, however restricted a group of the curious or the studious, the idle or the earnest, the casual vagrant along the fringes of understanding or the single-purposed seeker after knowledge?" The collector who conducts such an examination need not regard the transient occupants of his shelves as museum pieces in embryo, or put himself in the place of a curator who will not be born for two or three centuries. Above all, he must not, for his own peace of mind, attempt to translate his conclusions into dollars and cents, for that way lies perhaps not madness, but at least a woefully faulty and inaccurate gauge for the evaluation of his property.

For a book in a public collection has no dollars and cents value at all. It has usually been removed permanently from the market, and in the transfer it has surrendered all its potentiality for being measured by the market's standards. Examine carefully any noteworthy specialized institutional collection. Of perhaps a thousand units, all but ten may be commercially unimportant items that can be had in some bookshop at a few dollars apiece—and the eclectic ten may be items whose similars reach the auction room once in a decade, there to change hands to the blare of trumpets. Yet many of the nine hundred and ninety may be as essential to the importance and unity of the collection as its veriest prima donna.

Enforced economy introduced one factor into the library situation that is likely to persist. Librarians in the larger communities have come to the conclusion that there has been much needless duplication of acquisitions in the past. Take, for example, the New England city of A, which has an admirable public library and a historical society whose own collection is particularly rich in genealogy. The his-

torical society is not overendowed, but it has funds sufficient
to acquire such new genealogies as are published (it is
usually a long time between new genealogies) in addition
to the out-of-print compilations which it lacks. The public
library of A, which formerly bought an occasional genealogy
of strong local interest, buys genealogies no more. If a representative of the X family applies at the public library for the
X genealogy, he is referred to the historical society.

Such a concentration of reference collections has obvious
advantages to the student, though it inevitably restricts the
bookseller's market. But a ray of hope is discernible. Out of
such a situation may well develop a phase of selectivity with
institutional collecting that, initiated and prosecuted with
intelligence, thoroughness, and enthusiasm, could exploit the
potentialities of public and semipublic libraries, particularly
the former, to an impressive degree. The opportunities for
public libraries to become repositories of special collections
are not even limited to the number of libraries, for there is
no reason why one library should confine its activities to a
single field.

The capacity to absorb rare and costly units, whether the
absorption be by individuals or by libraries, can obviously
be impaired, but it can never be destroyed. What are the
limits of this capacity to absorb? Has it any limits? Certainly not, if one sets the selling price low enough.

Certainly some new libraries, both private and institutional, began to be assembled during the years following
1929—never was there a better moment in which to initiate
such a high emprise, and books, good books, continued to be
hawked and bought while cabinets tottered and tumbled
and gold was winning a decree nisi. For while overproduction of something or other may have been a factor in bringing on the cataclysm (though our weightiest economists say
it was not), there has been no overproduction of rare books.
Institutions which could not buy had rarities willed to them,

and a book bequeathed to a theoretically deathless institution is as definitely *non est* as if it had been flung into a furnace. Despite the recent laudable sales of surplus material by certain institutions, such action remains the exception rather than the rule, and seems long destined to remain so.

A rare book, whether it cost one dollar or fifty thousand, is a luxury. The operation of collector psychology, of course, converts it into something very like a necessity. The collector who gets the most fun out of the business is the collector who has to deny himself something to get the book he has to have, and there are plenty of authentic instances of collectors who have sacrificed trips abroad or foregone new cars in order to place on their shelves thin little pamphlets, each of which took up no more room than a shirt board. Gissing omitted a supper and bought a Horace (or was it a Theocritus?), but it was not Pine's Horace nor the Aldine Theocritus.

Nothing provides more impressive evidence of the tremendous growth of interest in the collecting of modern authors than a study of the familiar and useful *Auction Prices of Books,* edited by the late Luther S. Livingston, and published in four thick quarto volumes in 1905. As a practical price guide the compilation is, of course, hopelessly out of date, but it is still of value, and will always remain so, as a meticulous and comprehensive survey of the American and English auction field over many years, as a compact bibliographical manual, and as a means of tracing the history of specific copies of specific books. For it covers such a span of time that often a specific copy has several entries—thus the Ives copy of the Gutenberg Bible, with seventeen leaves in facsimile, which sold in 1891 for the then sensational figure of $14,800, had brought $8,000 ten years earlier, and the Bodleian duplicate of the Eliot Indian Bible sold for $1,130 in 1868, $1,050 in 1870, $900 in 1876, $1,250 in 1883, $1,650 in 1891, and £370 in 1902, by which latter year it had become the Bodleian-Bruce-Rice-Menzies-Cooke-Ives copy.

Such data is as instructive as it is fascinating, as provoca-
tive as it is provoking. Here are ten quotations of *Fanshawe,*
for instance, ranging from $75 to $840—the latter probably
considered an insane figure for 1902. *The Scarlet Letter*
ranged up to $32; copies of the second edition, with the new
preface, sold for the good figures of $7 and $8. The only
copy of *The Luck of Roaring Camp* quoted brought $6.50
(in those days auctioneers did not say "No half-dollar bids,
madam"); Bret Harte collectors seem to have been more
interested in *Outcroppings,* which sold up to $24, and in the
Chicago issue of *The Heathen Chinee,* several copies of
which averaged around $10. Longfellow's *Evangeline* sold
up to $137 for a copy in morocco; the best price for a copy
in boards was $91; presentation copies a decade earlier had
brought $26 and $31. *The Song of Hiawatha* could do no
better than $28 for a copy in morocco. A presentation copy
of Lowell's *Commemoration Ode* (1865) sold for $6 five
years after publication; subsequent prices for presentation
copies were: 1900, $60; 1901, $220 and $410; 1903, $400.

Only one copy of Poe's *Tamerlane* (which, rather un-
justly, has become the symbol of scarcity in original editions
of American literature) is recorded, but it was sold three
times. As the Ives copy, in the original paper covers, it
brought $1,850 in 1893. The following year, as the Maxwell
copy, now dressed in full morocco with the original wrapper
bound in, it sold for $1,450. (The very fine Frank J. Hogan
copy in the original paper wrappers sold for $15,500 in 1945.)
By 1900 it had recovered somewhat from the morocco handicap, and brought $2,050. The copy of *The Raven* which
Poe gave to Mrs. Sarah Helen Whitman changed hands in
1900 for $610.

But among authors who are classed as moderns (and who
in 1905, of course, were more modern still) a host are conspicuous by their absence. There are no Conrad quotations,

TAMERLANE

AND

OTHER POEMS.

BY A BOSTONIAN.

Young heads are giddy, and young hearts are warm,
And make mistakes for manhood to reform.—COWPER.

BOSTON:

CALVIN F. S. THOMAS.....PRINTER.

. . . .

1827.

Tamerlane, Edgar Allan Poe's
first book, is the most sought-for volume
of American poetry.

though by the year in which *Auction Prices of Books* appeared, ten Conrad titles, from *Almayer's Folly* to *Nostromo*, were available. There are no entries under Galsworthy, whose four Sinjohn books had appeared from 1897 to 1901, and who had already written *The Island Pharisees* under his own name. Both Conrad and Galsworthy, of course, were virtual unknowns at the time—actual unknowns to collectors. Barrie, however, already enjoyed a large following, and had won assured critical prestige; moreover, he had been writing for nearly twenty years. Yet the sole Barrie entry is $51 for a set of the Thistle edition on Japan paper, one of 150 signed by the author. But between 1888 and 1904 no one seems to have been interested in *An Edinburgh Eleven, My Lady Nicotine, The Little Minister, Auld Licht Idylls,* or the very rare *Better Dead.*

Shaw was already a great playwright, but a playwright whom nobody collected—his namesake, George Shaw, author of a 28-volume *General Zoology* (London, 1800–1826), was, however, represented. Mark Twain was esteemed only for his complete works and his first book, *The Celebrated Jumping Frog of Calaveras County*—of four copies listed one brought $11, and not one of the others half that. Apparently no one was interested in *Tom Sawyer, Huckleberry Finn,* or *The Innocents Abroad.* There are no entries under Stephen Crane, whose *Red Badge of Courage* was ten years old, or under Theodore Dreiser, whose *Sister Carrie* was a sub-sub-deb of five.

Hardy, Kipling, and Stevenson are represented in varying abundance. Stevenson items occupying seven pages, Kipling four, Hardy less than half a page. Of ten *Treasure Islands* offered one fetched $18, of twelve *Child's Gardens* the best price was $19 as far back as 1894, when the book was nine years old. *Departmental Ditties* was in good supply and good demand alike; of twenty-one copies offered between 1897 and 1903 (of which at least one was "without the flap") the highest price reached was £20 15s. Oddly enough, this copy was the earliest of the 21; 1901 and 1903 could show only $26 and $21 respectively. But even these figures were substantial for their era. It is interesting to note that the two *Jungle Books* (1894 and 1895) won auction recognition as early as 1899—£1 4s—and in the following year reached $17. The scarcity of the London *Letters of Marque* and the Allahabad *Smith Administration* were not yet appreciated—at any rate the appreciation did not translate into a large amount of cash. The former brought £3, the latter £26 at Sotheby's in December, 1898, compared to respective 1927 and 1928 valuations of $10,900 and $14,000. They have since receded from those high-water marks.

Nine Hardy titles won inclusion in *Auction Prices of Books*. Of four copies of *Desperate Remedies*, the dearest cost £6 7s 6d in 1901. A presentation copy to William Morris of *Tess of the D'Urbervilles* sold for £4 8s in 1898; crossing the Atlantic, it brought $15 the following year. It is time, perhaps, to draw the curtain on what can only be a painful scene.

Unless a person feels a definite urge to collect books as books, he had better collect something else. He should not collect books as merchandise. There are so many less wieldy things to gamble with, and will be while Wall Street endures and fifty-two cards constitute a deck.

There are, in conclusion, one or two minor financial considerations. In collecting books one need have no regard for overhead or upkeep. True, a book collection, even the most modest, should be insured against fire, preferably after an expert appraisal, but we can think of no other running expense. Thieves will break in and steal until the end of time, but, unless they happen to be themselves collectors, they are not likely to trouble about rare books, for few commodities are less readily negotiable when illicitly come by, or so easy to trace.

■

CHAPTER EIGHT

TOOLS
OF
THE
TRADE

■

A common question asked by the neophyte collector is: "Where can I find a work listing *all* rare books and their values?" The short answer to that is, nowhere. There are just too many books of value to be fit into one ready-reference volume. However, there are many more sources of information extant than the beginner may imagine. No matter who the author or what the subject he may be interested in, whatever the period or nationality, there is sure to be, somewhere, an account of his books. If one is interested in tobacco, there is the great George Arents bibliography, published by the New York Public Library. If it is vertebrate zoology, Casey A. Woods's *An Introduction* to its literature is available in no fewer than 643 quarto pages. Others are as diverse as L. C. Karpinski's *Bibliography of Mathematical Works Printed in America through 1850,* Pilling's *Bibliography of the Algonquian Languages,* and Reid, Habib, Jay, and Simmonini's *Bibliography of the Island of Guam* in 102 double-column pages. There are guides of some sort to every subject mentioned on page 55, and the collector should know and consult those that concern his specialty.

Not even the advanced collector need own such behemoths of bibliography as Joseph Sabin's *A Dictionary of Books Relating to America from Its Discovery to the Present Time* (New York, 1868–1936), 29 volumes, begun by Joseph Sabin, continued by Wilberforce Eames, and completed by R. W. G. Vail; or Charles Evans's *American Bibliography. A Chronological Dictionary of all Books, Pamphlets and Periodical Publications Printed in the United States of America from the Genesis of Printing in 1639, down to and Including the Year 1800. With Bibliographical and Biographical Notes* (New York, 1903–1934), ten volumes, with its supplement, *American Bibliography, a Preliminary Check List*, 1801–1819, by Ralph Shaw and Richard Shoemaker, 21 volumes, New York, 1958–1965; or Jacob Blanck's *Bibliography of American Literature* (1955–continuing), four volumes of which have been published, which lists works of a selective list of authors from the Federal period to those who died before 1930.

The prices books have brought at auction have been meticulously recorded, since before the turn of the century, in England by *Book Auction Records* and in America by *American Book-Prices Current*. As their titles suggest, they record all books sold at auction which bring a minimum of $5. Recently a new Annual has appeared which lists a large selection of books from dealers' catalogues, thus giving retail prices, whereas auction records are, theoretically, wholesale. This is the *Bookman's Price Index. An Annual Guide to the Values of Rare and other Out-of-Print Books and Sets of Periodicals*, compiled by Daniel F. McGrath (Detroit, Michigan, 1964).

Though the average collector need not own the above-mentioned works (indeed, their very bulk would constitute a good-sized library), he should know about them and realize that they can be consulted at any large library and many rare bookshops.

There are several book collectors' magazines to which attention should be paid. These include *The Book Collecting World* (913 West Cullom Avenue, Chicago, Illinois), a weekly; *The American Book Collector* (1822 School Street, Chicago, Illinois), issued ten times a year; *The Book Collector* (58 Frith Street, London, W.1), a quarterly. The most ambitious effort in America for a bibliographical magazine was *The Colophon* (of which John Winterich was one of the editors), 1930–1950, copies of which appear with some frequency on the market, and which can be found in most large libraries. It contains much useful and entertaining material, and would be much more useful if equipped with a full index. Autograph collectors should know of the quarterly publication *Manuscripts* (5733 Kimbark Avenue, Chicago, Illinois), a lively publication covering all aspects of its field.

But by far the most important periodical is the *Antiquarian Bookman. The Specialist Book Trade Weekly,* Sol Malkin, editor (Box 1100, Newark 1, New Jersey), which reports the news of new and used, old and rare, out-of-print, and specialist books. Here wanted books can be advertised for, unwanted books listed for sale. It is the most useful single current compendium the neophyte can acquire. Its annual "Bookman's Yearbooks" are practically-for-free encyclopedias of the trade and its vagaries.

There is nothing comparable to it in England, though there the august (London) *Times Literary Supplement* (weekly) devotes on its back page much more attention to book sales and bibliographical matters generally than do all American newspapers combined.

Much valuable information as well as infinite pleasurable reading is to be found in the writings of books about book collecting by A. Edward Newton, Vincent Starrett, Percy Muir, Holbrook Jackson, John Carter, and others who carry on in this twentieth century, in the noble tradition of the English essay, the torch of bibliomania.

The following brief listing of some of the bibliographies and books on collecting does not pretend to be anything but an indication of the richness and vastness of the field. Many of the works listed are, alas, out of print, but they can occasionally be picked up at second hand and are usually available in libraries. There are so many bibliographies of individual authors that none are listed. To the about-to-become-a-book collector, then, good hunting!

BOOKS ABOUT BOOKS

BURLINGAME, ROGER. *Of Making Many Books. A Hundred Years of Reading, Writing and Publishing.* New York, 1946.

CARTER, JOHN. *A B C for Book Collectors.* New York, 1961.

———. *Taste and Technique in Book-collecting.* New York, 1948.

———, ed. *New Paths in Book Collecting.* London, 1934.

CARTER, JOHN and GRAHAM POLLARD. *An Enquiry into the Nature of Certain 19th Century Pamphlets.* London, 1934. The famed exposure of the forger Thomas J. Wise.

EVERETT, CHARLES P. *The Adventures of a Treasure Hunter.* Boston, 1951.

GOODSPEED, CHARLES. *Yankee Bookseller.* Boston, 1937.

JACKSON, HOLBROOK. *The Anatomy of Bibliomania.* 2 volumes. London, 1930.

LEWIS, WILMARTH. *Collector's Progress.* New York, 1951.

MUIR, PERCY. *Book-Collecting as a Hobby.* London, 1945.

———. *Minding My Own Business.* London, 1956.

NEWTON, A. EDWARD. *The Amenities of Book-Collecting and Kindred Affections.* Boston, 1918.

————. *The Greatest Book in the World and Other Papers.* Boston, 1925.

POWELL, LAWRENCE. *Books in My Baggage.* New York, 1960.

————. *A Passion For Books.* New York, 1959.

ROSENBACH, A. S. W. *Books and Bidders. The Adventures of a Bibliophile.* Boston, 1927.

STARRETT, VINCENT. *Bookman's Holiday.* New York, 1942.

————. *Born in a Book Store.* Oklahoma University Press, 1965.

————. *Penny Wise and Book Foolish.* New York, 1929.

TARG, WILLIAM, ed. *Carrousel for Bibliophiles.* New York, 1947.

WEST, HERBERT. *Modern Book Collecting for the Impecunious Amateur.* Boston, 1936.

WOLFE, EDWIN, 2nd, and JOHN FLEMING. *Rosenbach, a Biography.* New York, 1960.

A FEW USEFUL REFERENCE BOOKS

SPECIFIC

Americana

ADAMS, FREDERICK B., JR., THOMAS W. STREETER, and CARROLL A. WILSON. *One Hundred Influential American Books Printed before 1900.* New York, The Grolier Club, 1946.

BENNETT, WHITMAN. *A Practical Guide to American Book-Collecting (1663–1940). With all items arranged in sequence as a Chronological Panorama of American Authorship and with each subject considered from Bibliographical, Biographical and Analytical Aspects.* New York, 1941.

BRIGHAM, CLARENCE. *Fifty Years of Collecting Americana for the Library of the American Antiquarian Society.* Worcester, Massachusetts, 1958.

Cambridge History of American Literature. 4 volumes. New York, 1921.

JOHNSON, MERLE. *American First Editions.* Fourth Edition, revised and corrected by Jacob Blanck. New York, 1942.

KUNITZ, STANLEY J., and HOWARD HAYCRAFT. *American Authors 1600–1900. A Biographical Dictionary of American Literature.* New York, 1938.

POWELL, JOHN H. *The Books of a New Nation: United States Government Publications, 1774–1814.* Philadelphia, 1957.

WALDEMAN, MILTON. *Americana. The Literature of American History.* New York, 1925.

WRIGHT, LYLE H. *American Fiction. 1774–1850. 1850–1875.* 2 volumes. San Marino, California, 1939–1957. Volume covering 1875–1900 in preparation.

WROTH, LAURENCE C. *The Colonial Printer.* Portland, Maine, 1938.

Autographs

BENJAMIN, MARY A. *Autographs: A Key to Collecting.* New York, 1946.

HAMILTON, CHARLES. *Collecting Autographs and Manuscripts.* University of Oklahoma Press, 1961.

MADIGAN, THOMAS F. *Word Shadows of the Great. The Lure of Autograph Collecting.* New York, 1930.

Bookbinding

Bookbinding in America. "Early American Book Binding by Hand," Hanna French; "The Rise of American Edition Binding," Joseph Rogers; "On the Rebinding of Old Books," Hellmut Lehmann-Haupt. Portland, Maine, 1941.

DIEHL, EDITH. *Bookbinding: Its Background and Technique.* 2 volumes. New York, 1946.

Illustrators

BOLTON, THEODORE. *American Book Illustrators. Bibliographic Check Lists of 123 Illustrators.* New York, 1938.

HAMILTON, SINCLAIR. *Early American Book Illustrators and Wood Engravers.* Princeton, 1958.

Juveniles

BLANCK, JACOB. *Peter Parley to Penrod. A Bibliographical Description of the Best-Loved American Juvenile Books.* New York, 1938.

ROSENBACH, A. S. W. *Early American Children's Books with Bibliographical Descriptions.* Portland, Maine, 1933.

Medicine

GARRISON, FIELDING H. and LESLIE T. MORTON. *Medical Bibliography. An Annotated Check-List of Texts Illustrating the History of Medicine.* London, 1954.

GUERRA, FRANCISCO. *American Medical Bibliography, 1639–1783.* New York, 1962.

Music

DICHTER, HARRY and ELLIOTT SHAPIRO. *Early American Sheet Music. Its Lure and Its Lore. 1768–1899.* New York, 1941.

FULD, JAMES J. *American Popular Music. 1875–1950.* Philadelphia, 1955.

WOLFE, RICHARD J. *Secular Music in America, 1801–1825.* 3 volumes. New York, 1964.

Newspapers

BRIGHAM, CLARENCE. *History and Bibliography of American Newspapers. 1690–1820.* 2 volumes. Worcester, Massachusetts, 1947.

Poetry

HAYWARD, JOHN. *English Poetry from Chaucer to the Present Day*. Cambridge University Press, 1950.

JOHNSON, MERLE. *You Know These Lines: A Bibliography of the Most Quoted Verses in American Poetry*. New York, 1935.

Printing

ALDIS, HARRY G. *The Printed Book*. Revised by John Carter and Brooke Crutchley. Cambridge University Press, 1947.

BOWERS, FREDSON. *Principles of Bibliographical Description*. Princeton, New Jersey, 1949.

LEHMANN-HAUPT, HELLMUT, in collaboration with RUTH GRANNISS and LAWRENCE C. WROTH. *The Book in America*. New York, 1939.

UPDIKE, D. B. *Printing Types: Their History, Forms, and Use*. 2 volumes. Cambridge, Massachusetts, 1922.

(VARIOUS). *Printing and the Mind of Man*. British Museum, London, 1963.

Science

DIBNER, BERN. *Heralds of Science*. Norwalk, Connecticut, 1957.

HORBLIT, HARRISON D. *One Hundred Books Famous in Science*. New York, 1964.

Sport

GEE, ERNEST R. *Early American Sporting Books. 1734–1844*. New York, 1928.

HENDERSON, ROBERT B. *Early American Sport. A Chronological Check List of Books Published Prior to 1860*. With an Introduction by Harry T. Peters. New York, 1937.

PHILLIPS, JOHN C. *American Game Mammals and Birds. A*

Catalogue of Books 1582 to 1925. Sport, Natural History and Conservation. Boston, 1930.

West

WAGNER, HENRY R. *The Plains and the Rockies. A Bibliography of Original Narratives of Travel and Adventure. 1800–1865.* Revised and Extended by Charles L. Camp. San Francisco, 1937.

This is the third revision of *A Primer of Book Collecting*, first copyrighted in 1926. A lot has happened to the book collecting world since then, and even since the publication of its second revised and enlarged edition in 1946. Among the most important events has been the founding of a professional organization known as the *Antiquarian Booksellers Association of America, Inc.*, Concourse Shop 2, 630 Fifth Avenue, New York 20, N. Y. This would have been of great value to our mythical John Smith when he began his quest for Stephen Crane, had it then existed, and it is of substantial assistance to any beginning collector. Among its useful functions is the issuance of a printed list of member dealers from all over America, listing their specialties, combined with an article entitled "Books and Values."

This is their Publication No. 5 and "is distributed free in an effort to give the layman an idea of what constitutes a rare book, how values are established, what you can do for yourself to find out if a book has possible value."

BOOKS AND VALUES

Reprinted by courtesy of the Antiquarian Booksellers Association of America, Inc.

A book may be rare but not necessarily valuable. There are thousands of *rare* books, of which there are less than 10 copies in existence, that are of no value to dealer or collector. On the other hand there are relatively common books and a few rather recent books worth a fair amount of money. A book's value is governed by three factors operating together: intrinsic importance, collector's interest, and scarcity. Generally speaking, the books which are sought after are first editions of great books in literature, art, and science, which includes discovery in all fields. These are source books revealing the development of man, and are of intrinsic importance, their values being influenced by scarcity and the demand for them at any particular time.

To determine the value of your book, consult issues of *American Book-Prices Current* which list the prices brought at auction of all books selling for $5.00 or more. These must be used with caution due to peculiar circumstances which might have affected any particular sale. Only the experienced collector, librarian, or dealer will have full understanding of these, although it may be said that a fair price can be determined if there are two or more auction records of almost identical prices. For more detailed information consult an experienced antiquarian bookseller who can give you an appraisal of your book or books for insurance, tax, or other purposes. His services, like any other professional services, must be paid for. The fee depends on the size and value of the collection, but it is safe to assume that the cost of the appraisal will be only a small fraction of the value. If the books are of little or no value, there may be no charge at all.

By antiquarian bookseller we mean a person who deals in *rare* books, *old* books, or *used* books. This type of bookseller has invested time and money in learning his trade and how to use the tools of his trade, the most important of which are *bibliographies*, or books about books or authors. Some are highly technical; others are checklists; and it has taken considerable experience to learn their use.

If you want to sell your book, go to an antiquarian bookseller, who will discuss price with you. For a list of dealers, you may write for the Membership List of the *Antiquarian Booksellers Association of America, Inc.,* at Concourse Shop No. 2, 630 Fifth Avenue, New York 20, N. Y. This is sent free, and lists more than 250 booksellers in the country. The *Antiquarian Booksellers Association* is a nonprofit organization engaged in stimulating interest in book collecting, and in the maintenance of high professional standards among its members.

Every bookseller is willing to buy valuable books and manuscripts for which there is a demand. The first step is to give him a correct description of the book in the following form:

Author

Title

Size (give size of pages in inches)

Binding (full leather, ½ leather, cloth, paper covers)

Publisher and place where published

Date (if no date on title, give copyright date on reverse of title)

Number of pages and illustrations (plain or colored?)

Condition (inside and out, state if stains and tears are present). The bookseller can then decide whether the book is worth anything to him and if so will ask to see it. It can be sent by insured parcel post (book rate) or Railway Express prepaid, and he will return it the same way if you do not come to an agreement. If the books to be sold are numerous and important enough to justify the expense, the bookseller will travel to see them. Before he can decide to do this, he must have a general description of the contents of the library (for example: Americana, theology, or old novels, etc.), a detailed description of the more important titles, and the approximate number of volumes. Valuable books must be seen before an appraisal can be given; pages have to be counted, illustrations and plates carefully checked. It is obvious that a valuation cannot be given over the telephone.

Importance of the condition of a book. Even in a book of exceptional rarity and importance, the state of both the book and the binding, whether cloth, paper covers, or contemporary leather, is important to its value. Any collector prefers a fine copy to a battered one, and a rebound copy finds little favor, except in rare cases, since *fine original condition* is the collector's choice. A loosened group of pages is a defect, but a more serious one is a missing page. A leaf should never be torn out of a book. Any deficiency reduces the value of a book, or even may make it worthless. Music books, children's books, navigation books, cook books—all material which by its very nature would have been much handled—can obviously seldom be found in really fine state. Old pamphlets in paper covers may be of value if they contain source material.

Value of single issues of old newspapers. Very few have value, and those of importance have so often been reprinted that the chance of having an original is extremely small. It is difficult to distinguish between a facsimile and the original. The Library of Congress, Washington 25, D.C., has printed circulars giving detailed information on "The Ulster County Gazette" of January 4, 1800, "The New York Herald" of April 15, 1865, Wall Paper Editions of "The Daily Citizen," Vicksburg, Mississippi, and 13 other often copied newspapers. These may be had free by writing to the Periodical Division of the Library of Congress.

Value of old school books, sermons, and bound volumes of Congressional Records. A usually safe generalization is that these have little if any value. This statement is sound, even though there are numerous exceptions. The Eclectic Readers of William Holmes McGuffey have been so publicized that there is a widespread illusion that any McGuffey Reader is valuable. When it is realized that their estimated sales were 122,000,000 copies, it will be seen that they could not possibly be scarce. There is a small market for the first editions of the six Readers which were published between 1836 and 1857. Also of some value is the first edition of Morse's "Geography Made Easy," published in New Haven in 1784, the first American Geography. Again, old sermons and religious tracts touching on famous events in science, medicine, politics, or other fields, including those of literary or dogmatic interest, are exceptions.

Value of old Bibles. It should be borne in mind that the Bible is the most frequently reprinted book of the Western world, and by its nature the one book most carefully treasured by its owners. In many households it was the *only* book. Therefore as a text it is not scarce. Many editions, even of the later 15th century, during the first 50 years of printing, are comparatively common and worth very little. Rare and important editions are easily recognized by the experts: the Gutenberg Bible, circa 1450–1455, generally considered to be the first printed book; the Mentelin Bible of 1460, in German; the first Bible in each language; the first polyglot; the first authorized (King James) version; the first Indian Bible, etc. Then there are *oddities* such as the "Breeches" Bible, the "Vinegar" Bible, the "Wicked" Bible, which command special prices for some misprint or curious phrase in the text.

Although of sentimental value, it is fairly safe to say of all the rest that they are valueless in the commercial market, and by this is meant anything in excess of $10.00. An exception to this might be if the Bible belonged to a distinguished or important family and has extensive family records written in it.

Consult: Darlow & Moule. "Historic Catalogue of Rare Bibles." 4 volumes.

Edwin Rumball Petre. "Rare Bibles."

Value of runs of magazines, "Messages and Reports of Presidents," U.S. Government Documents. For these we recommend a small pamphlet published by the University of Minnesota. This is called "Disposal of Unneeded Publications," and ably covers the entire field. It may be obtained free by writing to: Division of Library Instruction, University of Minnesota, Minneapolis 14, Minnesota.

Value of sets. The pamphlet recommended above includes an excellent description of these.

Value of encyclopedias. Sets of "Encyclopedia Britannica" published before 1911, the 11th edition, except the first edition, have no sale value. For subsequent editions, the value varies according to the edition and the physical condition of the set. Generally speaking, those published from 1946 on are the most desirable. This applies to obsolete editions of all encyclopedias.

Value of first editions. Generally, but not always, first editions are more valuable than later editions. In creative literature—fiction, poetry, drama, etc.—the first printed form of an author's work is usually considered to be the most desirable, but if the text is later substantially revised, corrected, or altered by the author, the latter edition may be the more desirable. Certainly the first edition of any great book in science, medicine, or discovery is more valuable than later reprints.

Which leads into the question of why a correct *point* makes a book more valuable. Identically dated copies of books sometimes vary internally, and these variations, called points have been used by some bibliographers to establish priority of issue. A misspelled word, a missing period, a dropped letter, presence or absence of advertising material on endpapers, different colors of binding cloth are among such indications. It is a refinement of the situation referred to earlier where an author clearly revised or corrected his text.

How to tell a first edition is almost impossible to explain in a brief space. An intelligent first step is to see if there is any statement to the contrary printed on the title page or elsewhere. By far the greater majority of books exist in only one edition, and only the most optimistic bear the legend "First Edition."

Another test is: "Was the book published during the author's lifetime?" This is not 100 percent safe but a good next step. If this is the case, look further . . . first into a bibliography of the author if there is one, and if not, into some comprehensive and dependable checklist such as:

Cambridge Bibliography of English Literature. 4 volumes.

Cambridge History of American Literature. 4 volumes.

Merle Johnson's *American First Editions.*

If the book is on a subject such as science, theology, metaphysics, husbandry, etc., find out if there is a standard bibliography on that subject which will answer your question. If it is not in English, consult your reference librarian or a bookseller as to its subject, and he will give you the best references. If these elementary steps do not yield the information you want, you should consult expert advice.

Value of illustrated books. Books with large illustrations in color, of flowers, birds, costumes, or decorative scenes, are of possible value.

How to preserve leather bindings. There are ready-prepared products on the market. Formulas are given in Leaflet No. 69 "Preservation of Leather Bindings," Department of Agriculture, obtainable for 5 cents coin from Government Printing Office, Washington, D.C.

Value of manuscript material. Individual signatures or collections of signatures, cut from letters or written in albums, are seldom wanted, although a complete set of signatures of Presidents is always desirable and signatures of Presidents on White House cards have a market. In general, letters, documents, and original manuscripts written entirely by or signed by those who have made a mark in literature or science or political life have value. There is, however, a demand for single letters, collections of letters, and diaries even when the writer is unknown, provided the material gives important new facts about historical events (such as battles of the Revolutionary and Civil Wars and the early life of the country through the opening up of the Middle and Far West). The value of all manuscript material depends on content, date, and condition, and a dealer must examine it before he can give an opinion on current market value.

How to find when an old book was published. Fortunately, most books are dated on the title page, on the back of the title page in a copyright notice, or, in the case of some very early books, on the last text page, in a so-called *Colophon,* where the name of the printer and the date of publication are given. In the case of undated editions, consult the catalogue of a large library, or consult a bookseller who will help you. Unless, in the case of American books a date is printed on the title page, a date of copyright merely indicates when a book was first published and does not signify that a particular copy was then printed.

INDEX
OF
NAMES
AND
TITLES